# Values and Society

HAYDEN
AMERICAN
VALUES SERIES:
*Challenges & Choices*

JACK L. NELSON, *Series Editor*
Department of Science and Humanities Education
Rutgers University

Current Titles:
THE RIGHTS OF WOMEN
Sylvia Feldman
THE ENVIRONMENT: A Human Crisis
Michael Piburn
DISSENT AND PROTEST
David Naylor
CITY LIFE
William Lowe
WAR AND WAR PREVENTION
Joseph Moore & Roberta Moore
THE POOR
Kenneth Carlson
URBAN GROWTH
Paul Wilhelm & Robert Torrone
VALUES AND SOCIETY
Jack L. Nelson

# Values and Society

### JACK L. NELSON

*Department of Science and Humanities Education
Rutgers University, New Jersey*

HAYDEN BOOK COMPANY, INC.
Rochelle Park, New Jersey

*Library of Congress Cataloging in Publication Data*

Nelson, Jack L.
  Values and society.

  (Hayden American values series: challenges and choices)
  Includes bibliographies.
    1. Social values.   2. Social institutions.
  3. United States—Social conditions.   I. Title.
  HM73.N46         301.2′1         74-16251
  ISBN 0-8104-5970-1

*Copyright* © *1975 by* HAYDEN BOOK COMPANY, INC. All rights reserved. No part of this book may be reprinted, or reproduced, or utilized in any form or by any electronic, mechanical, or other means, now known or hereafter invented, including photocopying and recording, or in any information storage and retrieval system, without permission in writing from the Publisher.

*Printed in the United States of America*

        2  3  4  5  6  7  8  9   PRINTING
        ─────────────────────────────────
              77 78 79 80 81 82   YEAR

*Design* A. Victor Schwarz
*Editorial* S. W. Cook
*Production* Irene Groff
*Consultant* Dr. Abraham Resnick

# Editor's Introduction

How old will you be in the year 2000?
How will the world be different?
If you could choose, what things would you change between now and then?
What would you want to leave unchanged?
Social problems such as discrimination, pollution, crime, and poverty are the result of decisions made in the past. Are there solutions for these and other problems? Will they have changed by the year 2000?
What new challenges are likely to develop?
What choices are now available?

America shares a dominant value with many parts of the world—the idea of a democratic society based on human rights and social justice. This is not always achieved, and there are many disputes over how it can be achieved, but basic documents like the Declaration of Independence and the Constitution express the strong belief that this value is worth the struggle against repression, ignorance, and intolerance. A democratic society depends upon thoughtful and enlightened citizens. The challenges of social issues demand critical inquiry. The choices involve consequences for the future.

The HAYDEN AMERICAN VALUES SERIES: CHALLENGES AND CHOICES presents social issues in contemporary society. This book provides a framework for examining one of these issues. A similar format is found in each book. Each includes:

- Case studies illustrating the issue by focusing on human situations.
- Factual information about the issue which can be used as evidence in making social decisions.
- Divergent views and opposing value judgments showing a variety of values involved in solving the issue.
- Futuristic scenarios illustrating possible consequences of social decisions in future human situations.
- Suggestions for involvement in the issues and the decisions.
- Recommendations for further study.

J. L. N.

# Contents

1. Cases ........................................................... 1
   *Cases of Interpretation: Which Is the United States of America?, 1   Over the Border, 4   Is This Right?, 7*

2. Sources of Values ............................................. 10
   *Values and Environment, 11   Ecology and Human Affairs, 13
   The Cultural Tradition, 15   Language and Culture, 16
   Body Language, 17   Symbols and Values, 20
   Further Readings, 22*

3. Language, Values, and Society ................................ 23
   *Social Functions of Language, 23   Labels, Stereotypes, and Prejudices, 25   Right and Wrong Language, 29
   Science, Language, and Values, 31   Evolution and Creation, 33
   Further Readings, 36*

4. Values and Social Institutions ................................ 37
   *Defining Institutions, 38   History and Social Institutions, 42
   Agents of Values, 45   Money, Time, and Popular Values, 47
   Further Readings, 52*

5. An American Tradition ........................................ 53
   *Unity, Diversity, and Individuality, 53   Migration and Restriction, 54   American Languages, 57   Minorities and Unity, 61   The Melting-Pot and Assimilation, 61   Minorities and Diversity, 66   The Bill of Rights and Related Amendments, 67   Further Readings, 71*

6. Different Cultures and Different Values ...................... 73
   *The Cultural Filter, 73   The Head Hunters, 76   The Mountain People, 78   Technology and Stone Age Man, 80   Political Values in a Modern European Nation, 81   Subcultural Values, 84
   The United Nations and Values, 85   Further Readings, 87*

7. Divergent Views of the American Character ............ 89
   *The American Character, 89   Conflicting Values, 95   Change in American Values, 100   Further Readings, 103*

8. Futuristic Scenarios ............................... 104
   *Under Control, 104   Public Hearing, 109*

9. Activities and Selected Resource Materials ........... 113
   *Activities, 113   Films, 116   Filmstrips, Records, Multimedia Kits, Film Loops, 117   Simulations, Games, 119*

# Chapter 1

# Cases

**Cases of Interpretation:
Which Is the United States of America?**

The United States as seen by:

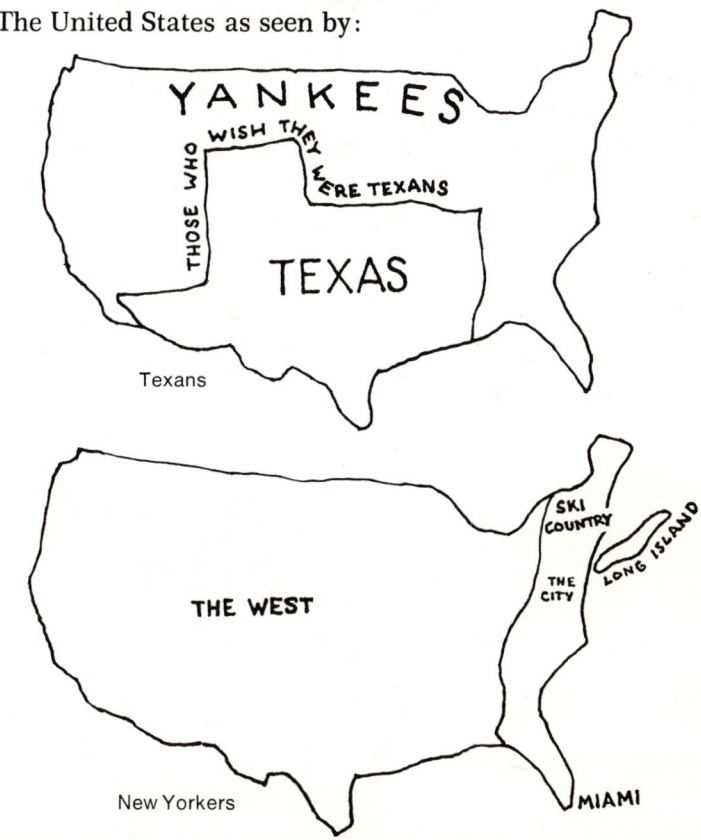

2  *Values and Society*

The United States as seen by:

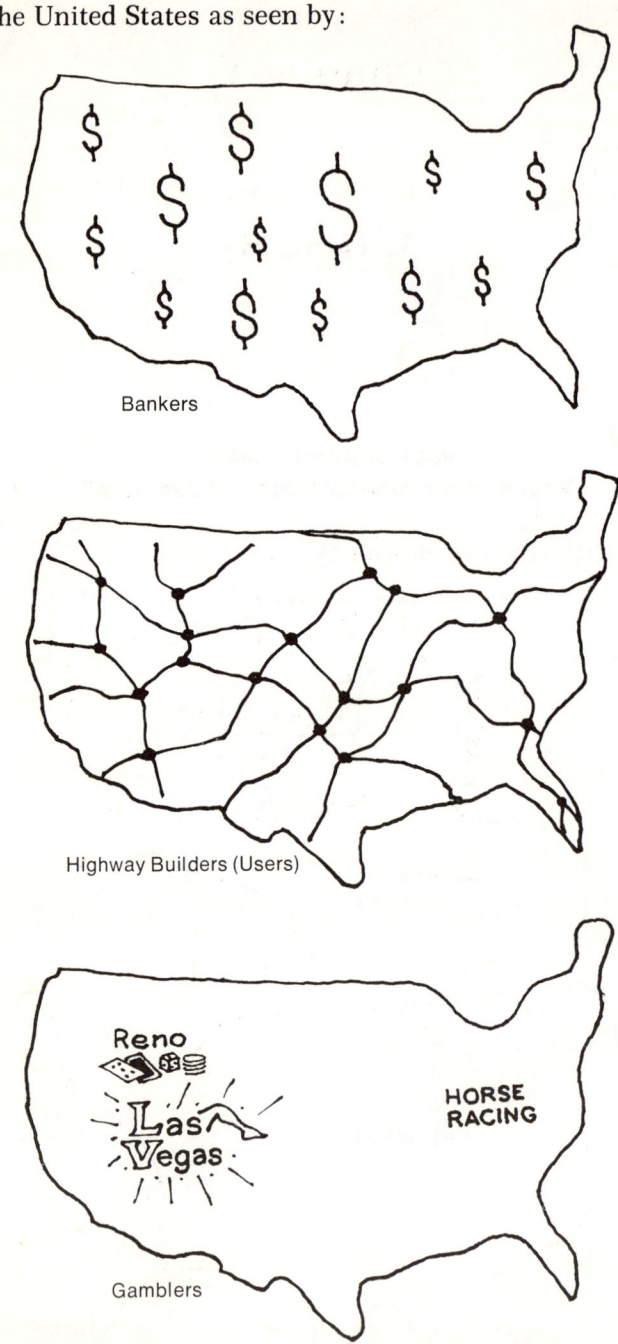

Bankers

Highway Builders (Users)

Gamblers

The United States as seen by:

What drawings might fit the United States as seen by:

Californians
People from your state
Environmentalists
Senior citizens
Children
Taxpayers
The poor
Women
City dwellers
College students
Canadians
Mexicans
Afro-Americans
The President
Russians
Movie theater operators
Door-to-door salesmen

How would you draw the world? What country would be in the center?

## Over the Border

The customs officer was leaning over the window of the car ahead of ours. In his gray uniform and cap he looked like a train conductor. The car was tilted slightly, giving him a clear view of the passengers. Apparently the concrete drive beside the customs booth was slanted. I wondered how many smugglers were caught by such clever thinking.

This was my first trip into Canada; actually, my first trip outside America. I was prepared to see unusual people, places, and things. The customs officer was to be the first contact. I was prepared for a customs search. The guidebook said that United States citizens had to carry proof of birth and that there were limitations on what could be purchased to take back home. I opened the glove compartment to take out my birth certificate and had to sort through maps and papers to find it.

The car ahead moved on, and the officer signaled me to take its place. He had not searched the other car. How could he tell they were not bringing in marijuana or some other contraband? As I pulled up I noticed the car did tilt on the slanted drive. I clenched my birth certificate and waited for the questions. I could imagine opening the trunk and sorting through my suitcases. I hoped Dave hadn't hidden drugs in his.

"Hello! Where were you born?"

The question stumped me for a moment "Denver . . . Denver, Colorado . . . United States."

"And you?" He looked at Dave.

"Kansas."

"Where are you going?"

"Uh . . . Toronto—for the National Exhibition."

"How long will you be in Canada?"

"About a week. We plan to come back Sunday."

"O.K."

He motioned us on. I felt neglected. No request for proof of U.S. citizenship. No suitcase search. No piercing examination of my motive for coming to Canada. While I hadn't wanted to be inspected, I felt somehow ignored by the process.

Dave had been quiet the last several miles. After we passed through the customs station, he said, "Why do they have to inspect Americans going into Canada? Or, for that matter, into Mexico or any other country? There should be free travel anywhere. A country can get rid of undesirables whenever they want. Why should plain old tourists be hassled at the borders?"

"I didn't feel hassled. The guy was just doing his job. Without border guards a country can't control the entry of foreigners. Criminals and spies could come and go."

"Baloney." (Dave, the cynic, had his usual last word.)

Memories of great spy movies flashed through my mind. A somewhat portly border guard peers through the glass of a booth beside a narrow road at the edge of a bridge. The striped and lighted gate is down. A long gray car pulls up at dusk. The headlights shine on the guard as he motions it to a stop. He calls to another guard in a language I can't understand. Both of them, one with a rifle, walk to the car. The fat one puts his hands on the driver's door and leans in. Suddenly, the door opens and closes, spilling the guard on the gravel, and the car jolts forward, smashing through the barrier. The rifleman fires several times, twice hitting the back window. A siren blasts and searchlights come on as two police cars roar after the gray sedan.

"I'm hungry." (Dave is rummaging through our food sack.) "Let's stop and get some chow."

"O.K. There's probably a grocery store in the next town. That's about 15 miles." So much for spy thrillers.

The grocery market was small, as was the town. Surprisingly, it reminded me of the places that dotted our road maps across Nebraska, Iowa, Illinois, Indiana, and Michigan. I guess I expected something different, maybe more romantic. There were some differences, of course. The road signs had crowns on them. Companies weren't "Inc.," they were "Ltd." And there didn't seem to be as many billboards.

Inside the store I recognized some brand names, but others were strange. Some of the familiar American labels, though, were printed in English on one side and in French on the other. Happily, I tried to figure out the French words for beans, flour, and soup.

"C'mon," Dave said, "let's get going. I'm tired and we need a room."

He had collected some groceries in a canvas basket and was heading for the check-out counter. As he placed the goods on the counter, he called out to me, "I've got some regular American food for tonight and tomorrow. We can stock up at one of the city supermarkets—if they have them here—for our camping."

The check-out clerk looked at him very coolly. "You must be tourists."

"Sure! We're Americans up here to go camping."

"Are you from North America or South America?"

"What do you mean?"

"Well, we understand that North America includes both the United States and Canada. You wanted 'regular American' food and I didn't know which America you meant."

Dave's face flushed a bit. He muttered something and then said, "Stan, pay this smart guy and let's go. . . . I suppose you Canadians will take our money."

The clerk smiled. "I'm afraid you haven't kept up with the news. There's been some problem with United States currency. In fact, the present exchange rate favors the Canadian dollar. If you don't have Canadian money, I must deduct eight cents from each American dollar."

Dave's agitation seemed to increase. I stepped up to the counter and offered some wrinkled bills. "Here," I said, "give me the change and put our stuff in a sack. Dave, why don't you go out to the car and I'll be right there."

It was Dave's turn to drive and he was at the wheel when I got to the car. His driving skill was not superior in usual circumstances, and now he was prepared to drive in Grand Prix fashion through a fog of frustration. This time I made sure to buckle my seat belt.

After a few blocks of sloppy, erratic driving, Dave started in. "Who does that guy think he is? He must not be the owner, 'cause he sure doesn't want business. I ought to report him to his boss."

"How about finding a motel or a rooming house? The guide book doesn't show any campsites around here. Maybe there's a Y in this town."

"Look at everything we've given Canada," he continued. "Did you see the Coke signs in his store windows? Almost every car here is American. Their magazines and paperbacks were from the States. I'll bet American tourists are the main source of income for most of the people in these little towns."

"Do you mean North or South American?" I asked innocently.

"Cut that crap out" was Dave's eloquent reply.

After some silence he opened up again. "We don't have to travel up here. Maybe we should have gone to Mexico or some underdeveloped country where Americans are appreciated. They don't even use English right up here."

I could see that arguing was useless, and I began to dread the week ahead. I could imagine a week with Dave's chauvinism in South America or Africa or Australia!

## Is This Right?

According to his statement before the committee investigating the Watergate break-in and related matters, Egil Krogh was given an urgent assignment of special investigation on July 15, 1971. Krogh was asked to take charge of a new unit established within the White House to investigate unauthorized disclosures of classified information. This special unit, later to be labeled "The Plumbers," was to find out about leaks of classified government information.

The event that apparently triggered establishment of "The Plumbers" was the publication of the so-called *Pentagon Papers*, a collection of documents relating to United States plans and activities in some key international affairs, including the Vietnam war. Continued American involvement in that war was being hotly disputed at the time, and the anti-war movement in the United States had become widespread. Newspaper publication of the classified documents in the *Pentagon Papers* occurred as a result of efforts by Dr. Daniel Ellsberg and others to make the public aware of military thinking. Ellsberg was considered responsible for the leak, and "The Plumbers," under Krogh's direction, were to investigate Dr. Ellsberg to uncover his motives, his collaborators, and his potential for leaking more classified information.

Krogh stated that John Ehrlichman, President Nixon's assistant for domestic affairs, had outlined the special unit's assignment and had given it authority to engage in undercover activity to obtain information about Dr. Ellsberg. Mr. Krogh felt that "The Plumbers" should "leave no stone unturned in the investigation of Dr. Ellsberg." According to Krogh, both Mr. Ehrlichman and President Nixon expressed to him their concern about the high value of national security and the need to stop leaks.

"The Plumbers" decided that some information about Dr. Ellsberg could be gained by acquiring materials that Ellsberg's psychiatrist, Dr. Lewis F. Fielding, might have. A break-in of Dr. Fielding's office was planned and executed. Mr. Krogh stated that he "received no specific instruction or authority whatsoever regarding the break-in from the President, directly or indirectly." But Krogh believed that such a break-in was within the authority given by Ehrlichman to "The Plumbers," and that similar operations had been used by the CIA and FBI on other occasions.

The break-in, according to Mr. Krogh, produced nothing, and he felt that it had been a mistake. He recommended to Mr. Ehrlichman that no other operations of that sort be undertaken. Ehrlichman apparently agreed and stated to Krogh that the break-in had been in excess of his authorization.

Dr. Ellsberg had been charged by the United States Government with theft, espionage, and conspiracy as a result of his activities in getting the *Pentagon Papers* into public view. When "The Plumbers'" burglarly, government wire-tapping operations, and other suggestions of improper government investigation came out at his trial, the charges against him were dismissed.

On November 20, 1973, Egil Krogh pleaded guilty to violating the civil rights of Dr. Fielding. He was sentenced to six months in prison on January 24, 1974. On the same day, Mr. Krogh issued a long statement about the case, his part in it, and his ideas about some of the values in American society. Included in his statement are the following comments:

> My experience in the months since my resignation from government, during which I have been under intense investigation and multiple indictments has also affected my view. I have throughout this most difficult period been free, first because I had not yet been indicted and later on recognizance. And I perceive this freedom as the very essence of our society and our system.
>
> This freedom for me is not a privilege but a right protected by our Constitution. It is one of a host of rights that I as an American citizen am fortunate to share with Dr. Ellsberg and Dr. Fielding. These rights of the individual cannot be sacrificed to the mere assertion of national security.
>
> National security is obviously a fundamental goal and a proper concern of any country. It is also a concept that is subject to a wide range of definitions, a factor that makes all the more essential a painstaking approach to the definition of national security in any given instance.
>
> But however national security is defined, I now see that none of the potential uses of the sought information could justify the invasion of the rights of the individuals that the break-in necessitated. The understanding I have come to is that these rights are the definition of our nation. To invade them unlawfully in the name of national security is

to work a destructive force upon the nation, not to take protective measures.

I see now that the sincerity of my motivation was not a justification but indeed a contributing cause of the incident. I hope that the young men and women who are fortunate enough to have an opportunity to serve in government can benefit from this experience and learn that sincerity can often be as blinding as it is worthy. I hope they will recognize that the banner of national security can turn perceived patriotism into actual dis-service. When contemplating a course of action, I hope they will never fail to ask, "Is this right?"

Chapter 2

# Sources of Values

We are products of two strong forces, heredity and environment. We inherit a variety of characteristics from our parents, grandparents, and others further back in ancestry. General physical structure, eye and hair color, and certain tendencies like baldness or long life seem to be inherited. Such innate characteristics are not altered by our social or physical environment. Certainly, a plastic surgeon can reshape a face and tinted contact lenses can modify eye color; but we are otherwise subject to the accidents of genetic structure for many aspects of our lives.

The gene structure carried through generations of a family may be called a genetic inheritance. These are characteristics that link parents to children, and lead us to observe: "He has his father's nose." "She has the same curly hair as her grandmother." "She and her mother look like sisters." "Their baby has the Durham eyes." Our personalities are not inherited as such, but personality is affected by physical traits that are inherited. Such characteristics as shortness or tallness in height, obesity, or a physical appearance that is considered to be beautiful or ugly contribute to the self-perception of a person and his reactions to others. There is a strong relationship between what we physically inherit and the individual and social environments we perceive.

Quite another kind of inheritance affects our thoughts, values, and behavior. It can be called a social inheritance. The kind of family into which we are born; the social, economic, and emotional circumstances of the family, neighborhood, and the surrounding society; the general conditions of each generation—all have an impact on how we view things, how we act, and how we live. Surely you are familiar with such observations as: "He'll be a drunkard, just like his father." "She has her mother's temper." "The whole family is rotten; none of them can be trusted." "He's got his father's eye for business." "They've inherited the national debt, the hydrogen bomb, and world-wide pollution; what more can we do for them?"

This social inheritance can also be called environment. While heredity may set limits for physical or mental growth, environment determines the extent to which a person reaches those limits. One may genetically inherit strong bones, but may develop rickets or malformed bones because of a nutritionally poor environment. One may inherit a tendency to long life and be killed in an automobile accident. And one may be born with a genetic trait like hemophilia, where the blood does not coagulate properly, but be raised in an environment which protects him from accidents and provides him with superior medical care.

At present, the relative affects of heredity and environment on intelligence are not clearly defined. Some believe that intelligence is primarily inherited and cannot be altered significantly by environment, while others believe that a capacity for intelligence may be inherited, but that environment is the major factor in its development. All researchers agree, however, that environment plays a role in what is learned.

### Values and Environment

Values are not inherited genetically. That is, we do not receive our values by some combination of genes before birth. Some evidence suggests that certain psychopathic criminals have a set of chromosomes slightly different from normal, but there is no general evidence that criminals, saints, cheaters, communists, capitalists, rich, or poor have any differences in genetic characteristics that would explain wide differences in values. Values are the learned products of environment. We may inherit a capacity for learning that limits the complexity of values we can learn, but the adoption of particular values is a function of our environments. This doesn't make it much simpler to understand how values are transmitted, though, since environments are enormously complicated, as shown in the following exercise.

## 12  Values and Society

In separate categories, list everything you can identify in your immediate environment. For purposes of this exercise, consider the immediate environment to be the room you are in. Use general words like "books" and "pencils" rather than listing each item like *Catch-22* or "yellow lead pencil." Use two categories: physical (those items you can see, hear, or touch) and mental (those you are thinking about). For example:

| Physical | Mental |
|---|---|
| Books | Phone call to be made |
| Pens, pencils | Sunday trip |
| Windows | Writing letter |
| Desk | Paying bills |
| Chairs | Holiday |
| Rug | Newspaper article |
| Noise from other rooms | |
| Family voices | |
| Dog's scratching | |
| Papers | |
| Door | |
| Pictures | |
| Radio | |
| Lamps | |
| Barometer | |
| Typewriter | |
| File | |
| Candy | |
| Shelves | |
| Globe | |
| Paper clips | |
| Waste basket | |
| Clothing | |

Was your list very long? Have you considered everything? Is this the only environment you have? Which of the items express something about your own preferences and values? Which items would you prefer not to have in your immediate environment?

Any person's immediate physical surroundings consist mainly of items representing his or her society, its values, and his or her personal preferences. Thus, a room in an American school will be different from a room in a thatched roof "school" in Samoa. But a schoolroom in Minneapolis won't vary much from one in Buffalo. Both will contain many of the same artifacts of western society—a clock, chalkboards, a flag, chairs, and desks. American students expect to sit in chairs, write at desks or tables, have electric lights, and live by clocks. Except where a society has been "westernized," these fixtures may not be normal parts of a learning environment among South Pacific Islanders. The immediate environment is a reflection of the society in which it occurs.

A list like the above is only a very rough way of approximating one's environment. First, environments are larger than any list of their parts. The general sense you get when you come into the room, while you're in it, and when you leave it involves many of the items on the list, but includes other less tangible factors like smell, your health, your mood, and the time of day.

Second, an environment is always in a state of change. As you began to catalog the parts of your immediate surroundings, you became aware of some you had not considered before. And this awareness altered the environment to some extent. Changes in air, light, shadow, dust, time, and personal feelings create other changes. Environments are interactive networks.

Third, the *total* environment is much larger in time and space than your immediate situation. Whatever happened to you just before entering the room, yesterday, last week, and over your life has some effect on your environment. Your expectations of the future also have an impact on where you are. In terms of time, then, the instant environment is partly the result of prior experiences and future expectations. In regard to space, the room is only a small part of a larger area: a house, a school, a neighborhood, a city, a region, a nation, the world, space. Your immediate environment extends outward beyond the room, and inward to your own self-perceptions and relations with other people. Outer space and inner space are important parts of your environment. If you feel crowded or lonely, restricted or free, your environment is affected, and it affects you.

### Ecology and Human Affairs

The word *ecology*, which has become a common term in the current social concern over environmental pollution, refers to the interaction of an organism with its environment. A Swiss biologist, Ernst Haeckel, originally used *ecology* to refer to the relationship among organisms that lived within a defined space and had developed patterns of adaption to their environment.

When the term was applied to humans it took on somewhat different meanings in sociology, anthropology, political science, and geography. Currently, *ecology* can mean the system of relationships among people who live in the same community. It can also refer to the interactions among different societies and their natural environments. Or it can mean the global relationships among population, resources, energy, and technology throughout earth and space. Our concern here is in human ecology as a major factor in influencing human values.

The recent energy crisis illustrates the relationship of ecology and human values. Americans had long assumed that oil resources were virtually limitless. Low-cost gasoline and fuel oil had led to dependence on the automobile as a dominant characteristic of American life. While environmentalists were trying to alter American attitudes toward the automobile to reduce its contribution to air pollution, the Arab-Israeli War of 1973 created an international political situation in which flow of Arab oil to the United States was abruptly stopped. Oil producers and power companies, under increasing attack by environmental protection groups and subject to ever-stricter anti-pollution legislation, suddenly found restrictions loosened and were actually encouraged by the government to turn to coal for power, a move that would increase air pollution.

The value of uninhibited oil consumption was altered, something environmental groups had advocated. Industry did not agree.

The value of strong anti-pollution regulations was altered, something industry had advocated. Environmentalists did not agree.

The energy crisis points up many value-laden issues: the interdependence of various nations; the relation of natural resources to human needs; the impact and limits of technology; the need for human adaptation to a changing environment; and man's intent to change his environment.

We are spending time on a consideration of environments to underscore the complexity of social life and the difficulty in determining exactly what causes people to have different or similar value systems. Though we understand that values are transmitted through our environments, we often cannot explain which values grow from which parts of our surroundings. An examination of the typical agencies of value transmission, however, does help us understand how the process seems to work. With some people, certain value sources are obvious. For example, a high value on sportsmanship may result from some particular youth activities or sports. On the other hand, one may value winning at any cost because of the repeated stresses of athletic competition. In either situation, the person may very clearly know the source of these specific values. More often, however, we gain values and modify them as a result of a variety of factors; and it is not usually until values are challenged or studied that we consider their sources.

In this book are discussed several of the factors or agencies involved in transmitting values. Although each is considered separately, they all form interrelated parts of an environment.

### The Cultural Tradition

Human behavior includes actions that occur instinctively, those that result from individual personal experiences, and those learned from others. Instinctive behavior is exemplified by such things as drinking, eating, and breathing, none of which has to be learned.

What is learned from individual experience varies. A fear of dogs, for example, may result from some particular childhood experience. In dealing with cultural traditions, however, behavior learned from others is the main concern. Children are able to learn complicated patterns of behavior from preceding generations. Each new generation profits from the accumulated knowledge of its ancestors. We don't need to test plants and animals to see if they are edible, or discover the wheel, or invent the washing machine because these accomplishments precede us and are retained by the human ability to transmit what is learned.

The sum total of remembered and communicated experiences is one way of defining culture. Thus, *social heredity*, as described earlier, is another term that can be used for *culture*. The word *culture* is used in different ways, though. In the broadest sense it represents the entire social inheritance of all humans. *Culture* may also be used to describe a set of behaviors and beliefs that are specific to one group of people. Therefore, our world houses many cultures. *Culture* also means sophistication or a high degree of education, but that is not the way in which it is used in this book. Finally, *culture*, in scientific usage, may refer to a particular strain of living things, like a culture of bacteria. For our purposes here, consider culture as referring mainly to the separate and relatively distinctive characteristics of behaviors and beliefs among differing groups of people on earth. Thus, *subculture* will refer to different smaller groups that share particular ideas and actions but generally operate within a larger culture.

Our cultural tradition affects the way we view any environment. We have been taught to "see" things according to the way our culture "sees" them. While there may be some individual or group variation, members of a culture will generally perceive events in similar ways. Their cultural screen sorts out parts of an environment by focusing on some and ignoring others.

The traditional ways in which earlier members of a culture have perceived their environment exert an important influence on what we see and react to. For example, many Eskimo maps of land and sea routes show distances only in days of travel, while U.S. maps show mileage. The Chukchee in Siberia identify 22 different compass points, mainly tied to sun positions and seasons, rather than our North, South, East, and West orientation. The Tikopians, island dwellers, use *inward* and *seaward* to indicate direction. The Trukese perceive fresh water and salt water as being totally unrelated substances; and Navaho Indians view the color blue as good and red as bad.

Describe a "warm" room in terms of colors and fabrics. Do the same for a "cold" room. What are the differences? Are there cultural traditions involved in these environmental perceptions? Which shapes are most pleasing? Which sounds and sights are most beautiful? Which smells are most delicious? The answers to these questions will differ by culture, by region, and by personal experience.

### Language and Culture

Major factors in the cultural transmission of knowledge include communication and organized society. Both are aspects of the total human culture, since some form of language and social organization occurs in all societies throughout the world. Language provides humans with a means for expressing experience in symbolic terms. We can understand what a Roman chariot looked like by having it described in words or drawings. We might also learn about it by being given a variety of parts and trying to put them together with no idea of what they should make. But individual trial and error, although necessary and valuable in many circumstances, lacks the speed and efficiency of language for conveying knowledge. Without language, knowledge would not be cumulative, and human culture could not have moved much beyond the knowledge of early man.

While the exact relation of language to culture is not entirely clear, and disputes continue among linguists over how man came to acquire it, there is no doubt that language and language differences are a prominent aspect of cultures and subcultures. Communication occurs through spoken and written symbols as well as by more informal expression such as facial gestures or other body language. We can, for instance, watch a baseball game on television and understand the messages exchanged between an umpire and a player who disputes a call without hearing what they say. If people from a culture without baseball were to watch the same event, their translation of it would probably differ from ours. In other words, the cultural context of the situation would not be understood.

## Body Language

The idea that body motion is a form of communication learned in a cultural setting is examined in the popular book *Body Language*, by Julius Fast. A more technical approach to this kind of cultural study, called *kinesics*, is described in Ray L. Birdwhistell's book, *Kinesics and Context*. Birdwhistell states that, ". . . no position, expression or movement ever carries meaning in and of itself." Instead, the message carried by body movements relates to the situation, or context, of the message sender and message receiver. For that reason, the cultural framework in which the baseball game is played and the one that surrounds the viewer of the game become very important.

Body language often exhibits itself in expressing the idea of *territoriality*, the sense of territory that humans and human groups have. Each of us has some notion of personal territory—a room or bed at home, a desk or chair in a classroom, even the air space that immediately surrounds us. This sense of territory differs among cultures and subcultures. Members of some subcultures don't enjoy being close together. Their personal territory is large, and crowding is seen as a threat to it. Other subcultures have much smaller air-space territories. Their members are accustomed to touching each other and being close and do not feel threatened by crowds.

## 18  Values and Society

Watch the body movements of people who feel their territory is being invaded. Usually, some physical agitation, facial change, and resistive behavior will be evident. After students have become accustomed to a certain seat in a classroom, sit in another's chair and observe the non-verbal reaction. What message is communicated? If a family member has a usual place at the table or in the living room, occupy it and observe body language. In a nearly empty elevator, stand very close to another passenger and note the results. While at dinner, move bowls, salt and pepper shakers, or other utensils into another's table space. Are they moved away quickly? Are there other manifestations of body language?

Body movements in one culture may differ in meaning from the same movements in another. The same, of course, is true in regard to subcultures and settings. Holding up a hand in class may signal the teacher that you want to speak, but holding up a hand in a downtown area may signal that you want a cab, or want to test for wind direction, or are pointing at something. Some subcultural groups hug and kiss each time they meet, while others are more physically aloof and separate. Hugging and kissing express different messages to close family members than they do to adolescent couples. This form of communication, body movement, is largely learned, and expresses cultural values. It is one of the ways we transmit and acquire these values.

A mother scolding a child can communicate meaning by face, arm, and hand movements, although the child may not be old enough to understand the formal language of the parents. If you have ever tried to communicate with a person whose spoken language was different from your own, you know the usefulness of gesturing. How many ways can you express the idea of *NO!* without using words? What gestures could represent the following English language terms?

Stop.
That tastes bad.
I like you.
Welcome
Don't crowd me.
Look out!
Four people

Which of the gestures above convey values? Do the baseball dispute, the scolding mother, or the gesturing for *NO!* illustrate how values are conveyed?

Written and spoken language also conveys a cultural content. L. G. Heller writes: "Every time anyone speaks or writes, he exhibits (a) evidence of the history of the entire culture to which he belongs, and (b) a total reflection of his own place within his own times." As an expert in linguistics, Heller is pointing out that language is more than just a carrier of information and ideas. It is also a way of examining cultural differences and similarities. Language, as John B. Carroll states, is a "cultural marker." It is useful in determining the boundaries of a culture area and in observing the movement and change among various cultures. Parts of the language of one culture become adopted by another, and scholars can trace these developments to assist in understanding cultural interchange. American forms of English contain words adopted from many other languages. This is clearly illustrated by looking through a good dictionary where the etymology (which lists a word's origin or derivation) is presented. The word *etymology* itself comes from the French language which borrowed it from Latin which, in turn, obtained it from Greek.

As words move from culture to culture and from time period to time period, they often change in meaning. The word *bedlam* comes from Middle English, approximately 1100–1500 A.D., and derived from Bethlehem, the hospital of St. Mary of Bethlehem in London which housed the insane. It came into general use in English to refer to any such asylum and now means confusion and noisy disorder.

Another example of meaning change over time and through cultures is contained in the word *virtue*. The Latin root word is *vir*, meaning man. *Virtue*, then, originally meant manliness. It later took on a meaning related to warlike abilities, and was so used in Caesar's *Commentaries*. It was adapted through French to English and came to mean also special or magical power as well as noble qualities. In common usage today it applies to goodness and morality, as in "Honesty is a virtue," which no longer fits the earlier meaning of warlike abilities. Also, a specialized use of *virtue* occurs in English, where it is used to refer to a woman's chastity, a considerable change from the Latin meaning of manliness.

Check the etymology of these words in a dictionary. Not all dictionaries contain etymologies. Ask your librarian for assistance. How have the values associated with these words changed as they have been used? In these and countless other words, the changes in meaning also involve changes in values.

20  *Values and Society*

arrogant      villain
cool          minstrel
companion     enthusiasm
gay           minister
civility      steward
vain          varlet
wanton        fuzz

It is easy to mistake the word used for the meaning conveyed. In this sense, there are no good and bad words, only good and bad meanings. Any word is merely a symbol attached to some idea or thing. The goodness or badness rests in whatever the word symbolizes.

When a word is used to symbolize something considered evil in terms of cultural values, the word itself gains negative connotations. Thus the word *lewd* once meant only ignorant and often simply referred to lay people's imperfect knowledge of religion. It has since become associated with a lack of sexual morality and has strongly negative connotations. *Harlot,* a word now used to describe a woman of sexual promiscuity, once was a neutral term, and meant a "fellow" of either sex. The opposite is also true: *Chamberlain,* now used as a very positive title of distinction, once meant room attendant. *Marshal* once referred to a horse servant, and *constable* was the attendant at the stable; but both terms are now used to describe a position of much higher status.

### Symbols and Values

Language is a combination of symbols. We use letters, each of which has some cultural meaning, to make words, and words to express ideas. But other symbols are also used to express ideas. These symbols, like words, may also convey cultural values. Some are heavily value-loaded while others are relatively neutral.

Rate the following symbols. Which are strongly value-laden and which are relatively neutral?

Sources of Values 21

Other symbols commonly used to express value include:

1.
2.
3.
4.
5.
6.
7.
8.
9.
10.

Which of these numbers do you think is the most valuable? If you were asked to rank these numbers in order of importance, what would your ranking be? When you rate movies do you consider some of them "first," "first class," "second-rate," "number 1"? How does your ranking of the numbers above change according to what is being ranked? How would you like to rank among people waiting to see the dentist? What number would you want in a lottery when the winning number is 6? What is your lucky number? What number do you want in class when the teacher is calling for student reports in numerical order?

⌈The social environment is a source of values⌉ This chapter discussed the interaction of people and things in the environment, and the cultural tradition that conveys sets of values to everyone living in societies.

## Further Readings

Benedict, Ruth. *Patterns of Culture*. New York: Mentor Books, 1946.
Birdwhistell, Ray L. *Kinesics and Context*. Philadelphia: University of Pennsylvania Press, 1970.
Black, Algernon. *The First Book of Ethics*. New York: Franklin Watts, 1965.
Crump, Thomas. *Man and His Kind*. New York: Praeger, 1973.
Farb, Peter. *Ecology*. New York: Time Inc., 1963.
Fast, Julius. *Body Language*. New York: Pocket Books, 1970.
Hall, Edward. *The Silent Language*. Garden City, N.Y.: Doubleday, 1959.
Kohlberg, L., and Turiel, E., eds. *Moral Development and Moral Education*. Cambridge, Mass.: Harvard University Press, 1971.
Kormondy, Edward. *Concepts of Ecology*. Englewood Cliffs, N.J.: Prentice-Hall, 1969.
Linton, Ralph. *The Study of Man*. New York: Appleton-Century-Crofts, 1936.
Maslow, Abraham. *New Knowledge in Human Values*. New York: Harper & Row, 1959.
Pyles, Thomas. *The Origins and Development of the English Language*. New York: Harcourt Brace Jovanovich, 1971.
Rokeach, Milton. *Beliefs, Attitudes and Values*. San Francisco: Jossey-Bass, 1968.
Russell, Bertrand. *Human Society in Ethics and Politics*. New York: Mentor Books, 1955.
Wilson, John. *Moral Thinking: A Guide for Students*. London: Heineman, 1969.

# Chapter 3

# Language, Values, and Society

What terms now in use among your friends have different meanings from those applied by other generations? How do these changes relate to differences in values of differing generations? How is language used in a society?

### Social Functions of Language

Language has a variety of functions in a society. It is used as a link to the past, as a way of preserving social cohesion, as a mechanism for communicating information, as a device for exerting control, and as an expression of social and personal values.

The link to the past has been briefly illustrated in the discussion of language and culture. In preserving social cohesion, language helps bind together members of each language group. Although language of some sort exists in every society, and thus is a factor in total human culture, language varies greatly among the different cultures of the world. This variation tends to separate cultural groups. European languages, including English, sound and look very different from Asiatic languages, though there are some common elements. Also, English differs from French, German, and other European tongues. These differences, along what are now national boundaries, assist each society in maintaining a sense of social identity. We expect people in France to speak French, in Japan to speak Japanese, and in Russia to speak Russian.

Many subcultural variations can be found in any language group, such as American English, British English, and Australian English, and within each of these are still finer dialectic varieties. Brooklynese, Bostonian, Southern, and midwestern language use in America differ enough to be evident to the listener. In fact, by noting word choice and pronunciation, some linguistic experts can listen to people speak and identify where they grew up. Such differences provide regions with a kind of subcultural cohesion. If two people from Alabama meet on a cruise to Hawaii, they are likely to consider their own common use of language as a bond between them. This is more strikingly evident in a situation where groups of speakers of different languages meet. They tend to cluster according to language.

Language is used by a society as a means for communicating information, exerting control, and expressing values. Information, in this sense, means the descriptions and definitions of events, places, and things. For example, we agree as a society about the meanings of *inch, quart,* and *pound.* Think what the building you're in now might look like if the architect, the contractor, the mason, the plumber, and the carpenter each had a different definition for these terms. We agree to use certain words always to mean the same thing to exchange information with each other. Our concepts of time, measured in minutes, days, months, and years; of place, measured by scaled maps, latitude and longitude, miles or hours of distance; of things—a book, a screwdriver, a doorknob—represent this use of language. The definitions differ among different languages, but the operation of a society depends on close agreement on the meaning of information-giving words within that society.

The social use of language as a device for control and as a conveyor of values is an especially important consideration in this book. Values and social control are obviously related. Social control requires decision about values. If we want to keep children from crossing a busy street, that decision is based on a set of values that the child needs protection and that the society needs streets. The crossing guard stationed at the intersection uses body language and sounds to exert control over both the children and the cars. The choice of a guard and uniform, the guard's choice of gestures and sounds, and the children's and drivers' reactions are part of a social control system and express values. If the society chooses a stop light instead of a guard to communicate control to drivers and children, it must provide some kind of instruction to both groups on the meaning of the lights. This, too, involves language as a function of social control and in expressing values.

Language can be used to persuade, praise, or condemn people according to the value meanings a society assigns to words. Advertising provides good examples of persuasive language using value terms.

1. Be the first on your block to . . .
2. Enjoy the easy life here in . . .
3. Deliciously smooth and creamy.
4. It makes you nice to be around.
5. Don't be left out. Buy now while prices are low.

Other persuasive language occurs in propaganda techniques used by groups to convince people of the rightness of their actions. Words used metaphorically often gain power and influence beyond their basic meanings, for they are used to suggest comparisons between the literal meaning and an exaggerated extreme. Examples of metaphors are: He's *over the hill*. She talks *in circles*. The price is *rock bottom*. This book is *a drag*. You're a *pain in the neck*.

Politics employs language to convey values. During recent national elections the following value-laden terms were used. Some were used metaphorically to show analogies between candidates and other culturally valued things. Some were used as code words signifying different meanings, depending on the audience. Which do you recognize? Which are metaphors? Which are code words? Are there differences?

1. A Generation of Peace
2. Busing
3. The Great Society
4. Peace with Honor
5. Right to Life (abortion issue)
6. Watergate Affair—Watergate Caper
7. Guns or Butter
8. Law and Order
9. Soft on Communism
10. The War Machine

**Labels, Stereotypes, and Prejudices**

The way in which words are used to express value positions becomes important to understanding language and values. Statements can be exaggerated, emotional, slanted, or relatively balanced depending on the choice of words. Because certain terms are culturally loaded, there is a difference, for example, in the values conveyed depending on whether we refer to a person who holds public office as a "politician" or a "statesman." We might also call him a "public servant," a "government official," or damn him metaphorically as one who "eats from the public trough." Obviously, each phrase carries different value connotations. A "juvenile delinquent," "young hood," or "misguided youth" may be the same person as seen by school officials, local residents, and parents. The "good student" as perceived by a group of teachers may be seen as "meathead," "butterfingers," or "pet" when viewed by others. On the other hand, all may agree on one value term.

This idea carries over into the use of language for social control, for the labels we assign to people and to thoughts and actions represent values. Which of the labels shown below match which of the people?

1. The President of the U.S.
2. Each of the two Senators from your state
3. Prime Minister of England
4. President, Students for Democratic Society
5. Head, John Birch Society

A. Reactionary
B. Radical
C. Leftist
D. Right Winger
E. Conservative
F. Liberal
G. Neutral or Unknown

How do you know you're accurate? On what did you base your judgment?

The labeling process operates something like the use of metaphors. Commonly agreed to, but often vaguely defined, terms become identified with certain characteristics. These characteristics are then symbolized by the labeling term, and that term is applied to people or ideas to increase their status (positive social value) or decrease it (negative social value). This is, in effect, stereotyping, where every individual identified by a label is assumed to behave or think in the same way. The label thus becomes a shortcut for describing the stereotype and denying the person's individuality.

Stereotype thinking, using value-laden labels, is what prejudice is all about—pre-judging some one or some thing. Prejudices are based on stereotypes and labels. Some of the labels, and thus certain aspects of the stereotype, may be based on actual evidence, but all too often labels and stereotypes are mostly inaccurate and convey values more than reality. Television's Archie Bunker exemplifies stereotype thinking with his use of ethnic value terms to refer to all people within a category. The Archie Bunker character has, in fact, become a stereotype itself, standing for people who are prejudiced.

Social control operates through labeling. We ascribe negative or positive values to labels and then use them in the media, in speeches, and in conversations to influence people about individuals or ideas.

*Example 1*

Anarchism is a theory that advocates the abolition of government. The basic premise of anarchy is that individual liberty should be the primary aim of any society; and that governments, by their very nature, interfere with individual liberty. Anarchism had been advocated by a group of Europeans and was adopted as a political position by some Americans in the 1880s. The labor movement in the United States was just developing strength, and a number of strikes had occurred. Some anarchists saw the labor movement as a means of destroying government and attempted to turn labor strikes into a political weapon. One such event was the Haymarket Affair.

In 1886 in Chicago an anarchist was exhorting a crowd of workers striking against the McCormick Harvester Company. When police appeared to break up the crowd, the strikers resisted and in the ensuing riot some strikers were killed by the police. The next day a mass meeting was held in Haymarket Square in Chicago to protest the police action. It was an orderly protest, but as it was breaking up the police appeared. Someone threw a bomb, and some police and strikers opened fire. Seven police and four strikers were killed. Public outrage over the event focused on the anarchists. Newspapers, speeches, and conversations labeled them as bomb throwers and violent people linked to foreign interests.

Demands for punishment led to the conviction of eight anarchists for the bomb throwing, although there was no evidence that any one of them did it. Four of them were hanged, and the others were imprisoned. A new governor elected several years later pardoned those still in prison because he considered the trial to have been unfair. Many people attacked the governor for his stand. *Anarchist* had by then come to stand as a label for bomb throwing and negative social values. The Knights of Labor, a broad-based union that had been under attack by business interests and newspapers, had very little to do with the Haymarket Affair, but the union was accused of being controlled by anarchists and this contributed to its decline and demise. Anarchist had become a socially undesirable label. Current dictionaries still include *disorder* and *violence* in the definitions of anarchy.

*Example 2*

The Red Scare of 1919–1920 and the McCarthy period in the 1950s illustrate how labels can be attached to people and ideas. *Communist, commie, red, pinko, communist sympathizer, fellow traveler,* and *dupe* were all terms used to describe and defame people in congressional hearings and in the national media. *Red baiters* and *witch hunters* were labels used by the opposition groups to describe those who were conducting investigations into communist activities. McCarthyism has become a label signifying tactics of public accusations against people by use of innuendo, association, and the denial of the rights of the accused to see and publicly confront the evidence.

The stereotype draws from Senator Joseph McCarthy's investigations into what he considered subversive activities in colleges, the military, the government, the entertainment industry, even the churches. His use of television to attract wide audiences, and his ability to effectively tie people to socially negative causes created a national condition of fear and repression. Individual careers were destroyed merely because some people used the constitutionally protected right under the Fifth Amendment to refuse to testify. Many writers, entertainers, and professors lost employment and suffered irreparable damages as a result of McCarthy's labeling activities during this period. This is a vivid example of social control through language.

*Example 3*

A third example in this area concerns the word "patriot." Prior to the American Revolution, a patriot in the new world could have had loyalties to any of a variety of nations: Spain, France, England, Holland, Italy, and Russia. As the new country developed, however, patriot came to mean a revolutionary rebel who wanted to break away from British rule. Thomas Jefferson and others proposed a meaning for the word which included the idea of continuing dissent whenever the government became oppressive. Thus, a patriot was one who felt strongly enough about the democratic and liberal principles on which the United States was founded to protect them against government actions that were considered to be against the good of the people.

Over a period of time the term patriot became identified with individuals and groups who felt that the United States could virtually do no wrong. To be patriotic came to mean not only saluting the flag, but also engaging actively in other practices that demonstrated loyalty to the government. Americans who disagreed with the government about the Vietnam war, the draft, and national interests were often labeled unpatriotic and un-American. Many of the dissenters used cherished national symbols to demonstrate their discontent with American involvement in the war. They flew the flag upside down, burned it, and spelled America with a K. Investigations and surveillance of these dissenters by law-enforcement agencies indicate the level of public concern over what was classified as disloyal, unpatriotic activity.

How do you define patriot? Which of the following are patriotic groups? How do you know? What are the criteria?

1. AFL–CIO unions
2. John Birch Society
3. Kiwanis Clubs
4. Students for a Democratic Society
5. Democratic and Republican Parties
6. American Civil Liberties Union
7. Daughters of the American Revolution
8. Socialist Worker Party
9. American Legion
10. National Organization of Women

### Right and Wrong Language

Social control exercised through language imposes sets of values on everyone from birth. We learn what is proper to say, do, and think through the language used to influence us. A father may smile approval and gesture encouragement as a baby learns to walk, or he may verbally chastise a youngster for using words the society considers to be profane or vulgar.

We also learn social values through the kinds of roles we are expected to perform in society, and through the language that expresses them. We are, for example, expected to observe the social values related to sex roles, and these are reinforced throughout life. The following are only a small sampling of statements conveying social values and sex-role expectations.

1. Boys don't cry.
2. Girls are so emotional.
3. Take your punishment like a man.
4. Why would a girl go out for football?
5. Barb can do the dishes, while Steve takes out the garbage.
6. I'd rather teach girls because they're so sweet.

We also use language as a control device for roles in other areas of our lives.

As a family member:

1. You shouldn't talk to your mother that way.
2. Daddy is very tired. Don't bother him now.
3. Kiss grandma goodbye.
4. Mary Ann is certainly a daughter to be proud of.

As a member of a particular socio-economic class:

1. Our kind of people don't do those things.
2. We must be charitable to those below us.
3. We can't afford to send you to college, so you'd better find a job.
4. If you work as hard as I have, you can be successful too.

As a member of a play or work group:

1. You're chicken if you don't.
2. Let Mike do it; he knows how.
3. When your apprenticeship is finished in two years, you'll be a journeyman.
4. He's dropped the ball four times. Let's bench him.

As a citizen:

1. A real patriot always salutes the flag.
2. Don't you have any school spirit?
3. I have rights, too, you know.
4. America—Love it or leave it.

These examples only illustrate the idea of language used to indicate proper social roles and, thus, to convey sets of social values. Each of us has many more roles in the course of a lifetime, along with countless other examples of words and sentences that influence these roles.

We learn through language a complex set of behaviors and beliefs ranging from simple manners like "Don't pick your nose" and "Use your knife and fork, not your hands," to abstract philosophical concepts. Each includes some value components.

### Science, Language, and Values

Values expressed through scientific theories tend to be more subtle, but relate to the acceptable beliefs of a culture. Scientific beliefs at one time permitted only the view that the earth was flat. Anyone who proposed otherwise was considered ignorant, unscientific, and, perhaps, even deluded. Now, science accepts the idea that the earth is spheroid. Someone proposing that it is really square or hexagonal would be scoffed at. The values represented in science rest partly on a set of scientific beliefs; partly on a cultural agreement about what constitutes facts and evidence; and partly on the language forms used in science.

Scientific beliefs prior to 1543 followed Ptolemy's idea fixing the earth at the center of the universe. Cultural acceptance established that the earth indeed did not move, and that the sun and stars rotated around it in perfect circles. Roman Catholicism and Lutheranism accepted this as theological doctrine, and dissenters who expressed different ideas were considered lunatics or heretics. Scientific language of the times assumed the values of an earth-centered universe.

In 1543 Copernicus, a Polish astronomer, published *Concerning the Revolution of the Celestial Spheres*, which argued that the sun was the center of the universe, a theory which provided a setting for later scientific work by Newton, and which led to the "Copernican Revolution." This change in scientific beliefs, or values, regarding the place of the earth in the solar system continues to have great impact on social values. Man and his planet had become less significant in relation to the universe. Furthermore, an increasing belief in the importance of scientific discoveries has caused a reconsideration of religious values in western culture.

The social acceptance of scientific and technological values has been virtually unchallenged until recent times. But the public is now becoming aware of the two-edged sword of science: internal combustion engines and air pollution; chemical detergents and water pollution; atomic theory and hydrogen bombs; computers and loss of person-to-person contact; electrical power and blackouts. In *Science and Survival,* Barry Commoner, a botanist and writer on ecology, states, "The age of innocent faith in science and technology may be over.... Are we really in control of the vast new powers that science has given us, or is there a danger that science is getting out of hand?"

He goes on to raise social value questions that implicate science in the making of moral and ethical judgments. After suggesting that scientists cannot remain aloof from the social consequences of their work, Commoner says,

> ... The moral issues of the modern world are imbedded in the complex substance of science and technology. The exercise of morality now requires the determination of right between the farmers whose pesticides poison the water and the fishermen whose livelihood may thereby be destroyed. It calls for a judgment between the advantages of replacing a smoky urban power generator with a smoke-free nuclear one which carries with it some hazard of a catastrophic accident. The ethical principles involved are no different from those invoked in earlier times, but the moral issues cannot be discerned unless the new substance in which they are expressed is understood ...

This reference to "the new substance" is related to the idea of language and scientific values. Commoner is here saying that the human meanings of science can be obscured by the complexity of its language, making its conflicting values difficult for the layman to perceive. To illustrate this, Commoner points out:

> Nowhere is this more evident than in the case of nuclear war. The horrible face of nuclear war can only be described in scientific terms. It can be pictured only in the language of roentgens and megatonnage; it can be understood only by those who have some appreciation of industrial organization, of human biology, of the intricacies of world-wide ecology. The self-destructiveness of nuclear war lies hidden behind a mask of science and technology. It is this shield, I believe, which has protected the most fateful

moral issue in the history of man from the judgment of human morality . . .

The conflict between religious and scientific values is expressed in the language used to debate the issues. One of the clearest examples of this value conflict is in the battle over scientific ideas of evolution and religious ideas of the creation of the world.

### Evolution and Creation

[The theory of evolution holds that plants and animals, including man, have undergone a series of genetic mutations over the millenia to adapt to a changing environment.] When, for example, the seas receded to uncover land masses, some aquatic life forms emerged from the water to become land animals. Over millions of years, succeeding generations of what were fish-like animals developed breathing systems that first permitted life both on land and in the sea, then gradually adapted entirely to life on dry land.

The concept of evolution is that of continuing change and adaptability. Some species become extinct because of inability to survive environmental changes, while others develop successful mechanisms for adaptation. In the early 1800s the French zoologist, Jean Lamarck, proposed the idea of adaptation through change. The most common example then used was the giraffe, which theoretically had been unable to compete successfully for food at ground level and survived by stretching its neck to reach food from higher locations. Over time the long neck became hereditary. Charles Darwin's studies of flora and fauna in the Galapagos Islands off South America led to significant modifications of earlier ideas of evolution. The publication of his *The Origin of Species* in 1859 stirred major controversies not only among scientists, but also between scientists and theologians.

The theory of creation held by dominant religions in Europe and the United States maintained that earth and all things on it were created by a supernatural force. This position in the Judeo-Christian tradition is best expressed in the First Book of Moses in the Old Testament of *The Bible,* commonly called Genesis.

The idea of creation as expressed in Genesis presumed that all living things were created by God according to His plan and would, therefore, not change and adapt. Each species is unique. Louis Agassiz, a famous Swiss scientist who became a professor at Harvard in the 1840s, accepted the religious interpretation of creation and was among the majority of scientists of the time who argued that the present forms of life on earth originated after a series of catastrophes caused by God which destroyed all life. He then created new life which He distributed over the earth. This was the scientific explanation for extinct species and changes in the planet itself. Thus, the values of science were at that time consistent with the values of prevailing religious thought. The first of Agassiz' ten-volume work, *Contributions to the Natural History of the United States,* published in 1857, contained his "Essay on Classification," in which he attacked all evolutionary theories by carefully explaining the classification of species and its consistency with religious thought. All species, Agassiz proposed, were created in their present form, locations, and numbers. Climate or other natural factors were not involved.

Darwin's book, two years later, challenged this orthodox view and set the scene for a conflict in values and beliefs that continues even today. This split between the inductively derived values of science, and religion, which draws upon deductions from faith in basic doctrines, did not start with Darwin and evolution. Leonardo da Vinci, Michelangelo, and Galileo each had difficulties in pursuing scientific knowledge in the face of predominant religious values.

Scientists in every period have differed on basic values like religion. Some, like Darwin, produce cultural conflict by using the scientific values of discovery and skepticism to unsettle the values of authority and religious doctrine. Other scientists have accepted prevailing religious values and produced knowledge consistent with those values.

The value conflict over evolution can still be found in American society. The famous 1925 Scopes trial in Tennessee pitted the religious fundamentalist, William Jennings Bryan, against trial lawyer Clarence Darrow over the issue of whether John T. Scopes, a biology teacher, could break Tennessee law and teach the theory of evolution. Even more recently, in 1972, groups in California demanded that schools teach the religious ideas of creation as well as the theory of evolution, because, they contended, the latter has gained a monopoly on the minds of the young.

The controversy arose over the selection of science textbooks for California elementary schools. In that state, local schools must select their main elementary-school books from a list approved by the State Board of Education. In 1969 the Board approved a resolution that the theory of divine creation be given equal status with the theory of evolution in the state science curriculum. The book screening committee of the Curriculum Commission reviewed books during 1972 in preparation for Board adoption of new science texts. Recommendations to the Board in the fall of 1972 included only books that contained the theory of evolution.

Most of the state's scientists, including 19 Nobel prize winners with backing by the National Academy of Sciences, argued that science and religion are separate parts of human knowledge which should be taught separately. They stated that only evolution should be included in the discussion of man's origins in science textbooks since there is no scientific support for the idea of divine creation.

The opposition, including the State Southern Baptists and other groups of various religious beliefs, argued that textbooks ought to contain an alternate idea to the theory of evolution. They argued that evolutionary theory—the idea of accidental happenings without special cause or design—provides an inadequate explanation for the beginnings of life. The resolution they desired was that science texts contain evolution as a *conditional* theory, as well as biblical accounts of creation, without any bias in favor of either. Opportunities were provided for scholars, religious leaders and others to present their views on the issue.

At the board meeting in December 1972 a motion to require that science texts include material on creation was defeated. Another motion specified that "scientific dogmatism" involved in the presentation of evolution be abolished. This motion would require that textbooks present evolution as an idea or theory, and not as fact. It passed unanimously, and texts which met this requirement were approved in the spring of 1973 for 1974 adoption by all California elementary schools.

What value systems are evident in this dispute? Do the divergent groups agree on the value of education? Why? What other resolutions are available in this conflict?

Another current value conflict between religion and science is in the area of environment. This conflict arises over the proper relation of mankind to nature. In Genesis is found the idea that humans were made by God in His image and were to have "dominion over the fish of the sea, and over the birds of the air, and over the cattle, and over all the earth, and over every creeping thing that creeps upon the earth." The idea of man's God-given dominion over all other forms of life has been challenged by environmental scientists who argue that the concept of dominion and the values it connotes for humans lead to misuse of the environment and a lack of respect for the ecological system.

Language as a form of communication expresses human values. Labels, stereotypes, and prejudices are evident in the use of language, and conflicts among people who hold differing values are conveyed by language. What conflicts can you identify in the speech and writing of people arguing about a local social issue? To what extent do they use the same words to mean different things? Do they use different words to refer to the same facts? What values are they expressing?

## Further Readings

Allport, Gordon. *The Nature of Prejudice*. Garden City, N.Y.: Doubleday, 1958.
Ardener, Edwin, ed. *Social Anthropology and Language*. London: Tavistock, 1971.
Bollinger, Dwight. *Aspects of Language*. New York: Harcourt Brace Jovanovich, 1968.
Boynton, Robert, *et al*. *English I* and *English II*. Rochelle Park, N.J.: Hayden Book Company, Inc., 1971.
Clark, Kenneth. *Prejudice and Your Child*. Boston: Beacon Press, 1963.
Dean, Leonard, and Wilson, K. *Essays on Language and Usage*. New York: Oxford University Press, 1959.
Douglas, Jack D. *Deviance and Respectability*. New York: Basic Books, 1970.
Fishman, Joshua A. *Sociolinguistics*. New York: Wiley, 1970.
Glorfield, Louis, *et al*. *Language, Rhetoric and Idea*. Columbus, Ohio: Charles Merrill, 1967.
Haugen, Einar. *The Ecology of Language*. Stanford: Stanford University Press, 1972.
Landar, Herbert. *Language and Culture*. New York: Oxford University Press, 1966.

# Chapter 4

# Values and Social Institutions

The process of learning various social roles, values, traditions, and behaviors is called by different names, including *enculturation* and *socialization*. Language and other communication systems provide one means for this socialization process; social institutions provide another. Language and social organization are not separate and entirely different agents of socialization, of course, since we use language to name and give meanings to social institutions. Language, in fact, can be described as a social institution itself. As Peter and Bridgitte Berger note, "Language is *the* social institution above all others. It provides the most powerful hold that society has over us." In reality, then, language and social organization are intertwined. They are separated in this book only so that we may focus on each of them.

Words and sentences are used to describe various social institutions like family and religion, and to suggest values given to them. For example:

1. If you think your brother is dumb, listen to what mine does.
2. Mother went to a meeting yesterday, and Dad fixed one of his usual hot-dog-and-bean dinners for us.
3. I think it's disgraceful to have church services at a drive-in movie.
4. Even the Rabbi put on tennis shoes and joined the basketball game.

Each of these sentences indicates something about roles and values in social institutions. Additionally, social institutions use language in different ways and change the social meanings of words and sentences. This conveys, in language, some of the values of the institution. In various work groups, one category of social institution, words have been developed or changed to have special meanings. For example:

1. Caring for the dead used to be done by "undertakers." Now they prefer to be called "morticians" or "funeral directors." The body is prepared in a "funeral home," kept in a "slumber room," and "put to rest" in a "memorial park."
2. Haircuts were once performed by mother, father, or the neighborhood barber. Now one gets "hairstyling" at a "tonsorial parlor" or "beauty shop" by a "stylist" or "beautician."
3. *Engineer* is a term with apparently high social value in our technological society. Thus, it has been added to many job titles to elevate their status: "sanitation engineer" or "waste-disposal engineer" for garbage collector; "learning engineer" for teacher; "demolition engineer" for house wrecker; "maintenance engineer" for custodian or janitor; and "floor covering engineer" for rug layer.

**Defining Institutions**

What about social institutions themselves as conveyors of values? *Institution,* as we use the term here, refers to an organized way of accomplishing socially recognized needs. When an approach to meeting certain social needs becomes customary, or traditional, it can be said to be institutionalized. A set of norms, or commonly accepted behaviors, develops around some social activity, and they are repeated again and again.

When people first developed the need to pass information and skills on to their offspring, it was enough that children were taught to hunt, fish, and prepare food. But as life became more complex, parents alone could no longer pass on the society's full cultural heritage to their offspring. To explain such awesome puzzles as lightning, death, man's origins, and the gods, tribal priests were required. Chiefs organized ways of dealing with other tribes and controlling members of their own groups. Trading systems and divisions of labor were gradually established. Some people grew food, others marketed it: some made things, and others provided services. As these and other human activities became customary, traditional ways of conducting social life, they grew into institutions.

Families, education, religion, government, and economics have thus been institutionalized. They may change dramatically from time to time, but they remain accepted social institutions.

Institutions are not specific groups in a particular location. They are broad categories of groups which fulfill social desires. Although we often refer to a particular place, such as a school, a hospital, or a prison, as being an institution, social scientists use a broader definition. Social institutions have no specific address. Therefore, an organization like the United Automobile Workers or the Saturday Movie Club at the Bijou Theater are only parts or examples of broad social institutions.

There are many ways of defining institutions of a society. For our purposes the definition can be drawn from *Sociological Perspectives in Education*, by Jack Nelson and Frank Besag: "An institution is any belief, construct, organization or being which, through historical circumstances, has become identified with a certain set of functions and behaviors."

Institutions have:

1. Functions
2. Actors
3. Relation to a larger society
4. Structure
5. Sanctions
6. Resistance to change
7. Status

*Functions* refer to those things an institution is expected to do. The police, for example, have the social function of controlling crime, and they perform this function in a number of ways.

*Actors* are those who perform functions according to traditional roles. In a family, mother and father assume the role of parents in relation to their children, and also function in other roles as children of their parents, as well as uncles, aunts, cousins, nieces, and nephews in the extended family.

*Relation to a larger society* means simply that institutions share in the broader general traditions and values of the society in which they exist. Schools, organized religions, and government, among other institutions, don't exist separately from a society.

*Structure* refers to a recognizable organization, either formal or informal. State government is made up of such formal divisions as governor, legislature, courts, and various state agencies, whereas lobby groups, lawyers, friendships, and family ties are informal.

*Sanctions* represent the power of the institution to reward or punish its actors. In prisons the guards have certain privileges, but run the risk of such sanctions as dismissal or suspension. The inmates can become trustees or be put into solitary depending on their institutional behavior.

*Resistance to change* indicates the strength of tradition. Before 1939 television did not exist as an institution. Then, after an initial period of great experimentation, TV became a very important, tightly structured influence in America. It has now become an institution firmly resistant to change because of vested interests and proven formulas for influencing viewership. Even the annual program changes follow socially expected patterns.

*Status* refers to an institution's ability to convey levels of social respectability to its actors. Armies give positive and negative social status to their soldiers. Industries and clubs assign status by awarding titles of president, chairman, etc. And schools convey status by grade levels (seniors, sophomores, sixth graders) and with diplomas and degrees; and by school-measured achievements (honors, class, valedictorian, second-stringer, slow student, drum majorette, etc.).

It would be impossible to list every significant social institution that conforms to our definition. Instead, we have gathered below general categories of important social institutions that provide for the transmission of cultural values, along with examples of memberships.

1. Family (parents, in-laws, sisters, brothers, guardians)
2. Peer Group
    (a) Age (12-year-olds, adolescents, elderly, middle-aged)
    (b) Sex (male, female)
    (c) Ethnicity (Mexican, Indian, Black, Italian, Greek)
    (d) Geography (neighborhood, town, region, country)
    (e) Work (plumbers, students, housewives, secretaries, lawyers)
    (f) Play (bowlers, model-plane builders, gang, friends)
3. Religion (Mormon, Catholic, Unitarian, Jewish, Moslem, atheist)
4. Media (TV, radio, papers, magazines, books, films)
5. Education (schools, apprenticeships, libraries, museums)
6. Legal-political (police, fire, government, prisons, military, courts)

7. Economic (business, taxes, money, welfare)
8. Medical (doctors, hospitals, veterinarians, morticians)
9. Organizational (Sierra Club, Rotary, KKK, Black Panthers)
10. Aesthetic (artists, writers, sculptors, architects)

Systems of social control, through the kinds of institutions noted above, are important to the survival of societies. They are not merely arbitrary social organizations designed to perform specific social duties, like street-cleaning, but they also express two kinds of values.

1. The values of social continuity and cohesion.
2. The values of expected behavior.

Social continuity and cohesion refer to the need for common agreement among members of a society about what ought to be done and how to do it. These are expressed as social goals that may never be achieved, since they depend on the process of reaching some sort of mutual understanding about what is good for a society. The present arguments over environmental pollution illustrate this process. The society presumably desires clean air and water, yet it also desires automobiles and cheap sources of energy. Each goal represents a strong value in American society. It is unlikely that we would use the institution of law to abolish the institution of automobile manufacturing because such an action would create a dramatic disruption in the continuity of the society's economic institutions.

This particular conflict is typical of the balance and tension in relations among many social institutions. The continuity and cohesion idea in this situation is that the auto industry provides jobs and transportation, while a good environment provides health and beauty. Both are necessary in American society since we have a set of social values that gives priority to paid work, money, mobility, and material possessions. Yet we have also been developing strong social values that support the protection of the environment to provide for society's continuity. We, then, establish some sort of regulatory system through legal-political institutions to try to balance economic values in auto production with medical or aesthetic values in environmental improvement. Social cohesion occurs as groups reach mutual agreements on what social institutions should be supported strongly and which should not.

Religions represent, typically, a stable and long-term set of beliefs that carry over from generation to generation. A child brought up in a certain religion learns a specific set of beliefs and ceremonies relating to that religion. These have been passed from generation to generation, and thus represent a continuity of belief, and are highly resistant to change. New religions arise because dissident groups within older religions find a need to change that is not shared with the original group. The set of beliefs and rituals becomes a means of identification of individuals with the religion and, thus, gives social cohesion among members.

Where a country has a dominant religion, such as Catholicism in South American nations or Judaism in Israel, the basic values of the nation and the religion tend to be consistent. Obviously, the fact that religions do provide continuity and cohesion among members through beliefs and ceremonies is a factor in civil and international strife and has often given rise to wars and political manipulations based on religious differences between groups. The continuity and cohesion of one religious group is threatened by, or threatens, another. The Crusades, the establishment of Israel, and battles in Northern Ireland in the 1970s —these are examples of the intensity of religion as a social institution.

### History and Social Institutions

The study of history is mainly an examination of continuity in social institutions. Typically, history books strive to show the institutional threads that weave through periods of time, with the concepts of civilization and progress represented by changes in social institutions during their development. The reason behind the requirement that students take American History in schools, for example, is that all citizens will be exposed to this nation's concepts of social continuity. Laws and regulations relating to the teaching of American History are based on nationalistic ideas that assume that the learning materials and methods used will show students how American institutions are an improvement over those of previous nations, and that students will develop a sense of loyalty to these institutions. The intent is to build a national unity, using the educational institution to strengthen a knowledge of social continuity.

Examine textbooks used in history courses. In the table of contents and the index you can expect to find considerable space devoted to such broad institutions as:

Families
Religion

Science and Technology
Business/Capitalism
Democratic Government
Transportation Systems
Communication Systems
War
Diplomacy
Education
Slavery
Agriculture
Labor/Unions

And within each of these broad institutions are included many specific social institutions such as schools and colleges, courts, international treaty systems, armies, and unions.

Examine the textbook treatment of these institutions to see what social values are conveyed. What social continuity and cohesion viewpoints are expressed? Are you able to detect the author's hierarchy of values?

In addition to social continuity and cohesion, institutions also express values expected in individual and group behavior. A neighborhood, which is a peer group based on geography, exerts influence on those who live there, communicating individual expectations to its members through various techniques.

Consider this case:

It was a bright Sunday in July. I got up early because Roger, Eric, and I were going to try fishing off the bridge again. We had talked about it yesterday and decided to see if the fish were biting early in the morning. Since none of us had been fishing much, we hadn't been too sure of when to go . . . or what to do, in fact. We had tried it one day after school in June, and got nothing. Then Roger had gone on vacation with his family and just got back on Friday. Eric's mom made him go to summer school to make up a D in math and had made him promise not to hang around with me until his summer-school grades had shown improvement. She still blamed me for his not doing his homework!

That's stupid! He could have done it if he wanted to and if she hadn't bugged him. In fact, he came over to my house all the time just to escape. We spent a lot of time wandering the streets and reading the magazines at Old Man Carlson's store. We could usually sneak in a half-hour's reading before he ran us out.

Most of Carlson's magazines are pretty tame, but he keeps some behind the counter and only sells them to special customers. I imagine they're really wild, like the ones Cliff used to bring to school. Cliff said his dad got them in the mail, and one day Miss Murphy, who lives in the next apartment, got a copy by mistake, opened it without reading the address label, and got the shock of her life. She told most of the people in the building, and Cliff's dad is afraid to talk to them.

Anyway, Eric was going to get out of his house early to meet Roger and me at the bridge. He didn't want to meet on the corner because someone might see us together and tell his mother. I had agreed to stop by Roger's house at six, but I overslept; it was already just about six. And I still needed to borrow some equipment from the Reardons next door. All I had was some old bait and a pole. Mr. Reardon had loaned me his tackle box last time and said I could use it whenever I wanted. When I tried to call him the night before, he couldn't talk because they were having a party, so he said to call back. They do have some parties. Mom and Mrs. Bardon count the bottles in the Reardon trash cans after each weekend to see how big the party was. They compare notes down at the beauty shop. I suppose if you wanted to know anything about anybody, you'd just need to have a microphone installed at Eloise's Beauty Shop.

There I was at 6:00 A.M. on this great Sunday morning, just ready to call Roger and Mr. Reardon, when the dog started barking at something outdoors. Mom woke up and heard me dialing.

"You can't call someone at this time of day!" she said in her strongest early-morning voice.

I stopped dialing and started to explain what we were going to do. Mom noted that I had not told her the night before, and that Roger's parents would not want to be awakened this early on a Sunday. She really exploded about calling Mr. Reardon, and gave me a lecture on disturbing people. I weakened under her attack, though I protested that calling Roger was O.K. Mom said to wait a minute, and then she got Dad up to talk to me. Dad doesn't usually say much, but he hates to get up in the morning, so I expected trouble.

"Nobody gets up at this hour on Sunday," Dad started, "we respect each other's privacy and quiet. If you had let Roger's folks know last night, they wouldn't mind, but you can't call now. Besides, you aren't going to run off this morning until the lawn is mowed. We have the only house on the block that didn't get mowed last week. Mrs. Durham has already complained that dandelion seeds blow into her yard if they're not taken care of. The rest of the kids around here seem to be able to get their lawns mowed each week."

My response was less than inspired. "I can't mow because it's too early, and people are sleeping. I guess I'll go back to my room."

Dad, slightly annoyed, but still victorious, started for the door to see if the paper had been delivered. Of course, it was too early for that, but I was still amused to see him pull his robe over his pajamas and inch open the door, peering out, to make sure none of the neighbors saw him dressed that way, while he searched the porch for the nonexistent paper.

What institutions are suggested in this case? What values are being expressed? How are they related to expected personal behavior? To what extent is the narrator of the story influenced by his family, friends, and neighborhood? To what extent do you suppose they are influenced by him? What would the story be like if it was told by the father, or Roger, or another character?

## Agents of Values

In the process of socialization—the development of basic social ideas and behaviors through interaction with the environment—the family is primary. It is the first location of human interaction; the first world that a child knows; and therefore the most important agent for the initiation of values. In a family setting the child learns habits and feelings that are appropriate to his own family as well as to the society.

The family is an essential social organization, since babies are born without the capacity to fend for themselves. The family has the child first. It continues, typically, to retain a direct relation to the child throughout the growing years. The satisfaction of most needs like food, love, and security is connected with the family in early years. And the family gives a social linkage system of identification by providing names and relations that are known to others: "Mary Brown, Bill's sister, has been the outstanding swimmer in our summer program." "Nancy's mother will be waiting for her."

Families are defined differently in different cultures, and family members may have different roles, but the idea of family is a universal social institution.

Much of the value system we hold comes to us through our family. Young children tend to accept the values of their parents, although during adolescence it is fairly common for youths to question family values and to rebel against some of them. This is partly the result of interaction with other socialization agents which have different values.

Peer-group values become strong as a child matures, and they may conflict with family values. Sharing the values of friends is seen as more important than continuing the values of family. The more divergent the peer values are from family values, the higher the degree of conflict.

What kind of music is valued by family as compared with the kinds valued by friends? What degree of honesty, integrity, and justice are expected in family and among friends? Typically, the adolescent period is a time of questioning and examining values. As they become aware of value conflicts, young people want to assess the differences. They may experiment with different value hierarchies to find a comfortable one. This does not, usually, amount to a total rejection of family or peer-group values, but is, rather, an exploration which may frustrate both parents and friends.

Families and peer groups aren't the only strong agents of socialization. The various institutions with which a person comes in contact express values and to varying degrees affect one's beliefs. Schools are obviously important agents. From age 5 to 18, school involves virtually everyone 5 to 6 hours a day for half of each year. Much of this time is spent in expressing the value system of a school to its students. What subjects are most important, what rules must be followed, what student behavior is expected, which students get rewarded, which get punished, and which get ignored are all part of this expression.

Mass media are increasingly important agents of values learning. Newspapers, popular books, and magazines are among the most influential of mass media, and help shape people's values. Through decisions on which news stories to feature, what topics and viewpoints deserve editorials, and what kinds of people are the heroes or slobs of society, the printed word assists people in making value judgments.

Stories about crime in the streets lead to public concern about safety and police. Stories about prison life lead to a concern for humane treatment for criminals. Newspaper treatments of wars, politicians, foreign countries, local issues, and everyday events color our perceptions of things. In countries where the government is afraid of free, public debate, newspapers, magazines, and books are controlled because the government recognizes the media's power of printed material. These same media are used to persuade the public that the values held by the government are worthy.

Radio and television added significantly to the ability of mass media to convey values to people. In recent years television has established itself as a strong socialization agent, a fact exploited by advertising agencies. There is something unusually persuasive about televised commercials that creates a major market for products that appeal to a variety of personal, group, or social values.

Television coverage of such events as the Vietnam war, the McCarthy Hearings in the 1950s, racial demonstrations, and the Watergate Hearings, stimulates broad public value questions. Instant communication with millions of people, in addition to the sense of reality and personal involvement that is more strongly conveyed by TV than by other media, has made the television industry a major socializing influence.

What image do you have of a doctor, or lawyer, or detective? Where did you get this image? Some will identify a relative, or a book or a personal experience as the source of images, but many will identify a character from television.

If you were asked to list the 10 most important social issues of today, what would you list? What would you identify as the main source of your ideas about existing social problems? Is it family, friends, newspapers, or television?

## Money, Time, and Popular Values

A look at the money allocated to different parts of society gives another indication of national values. Money is only a symbol, a medium of exchange indicating the economic worth of goods or services. There are other standards of worth, of course. Some things or people or ideas are measured in terms beyond monetary value, as when a person sacrifices success or wealth to stand up for a principle. If you were asked to place a monetary value on your best friend, or closest relative, or an important part of your body, you would have great difficulty because these tend to exceed monetary consideration. But, while money is not the only measure of worth, it can be used as one of the general indicators of values. Time, in American society, is similar to money. We don't want to waste it; we "spend" it; we make choices about how we can best use it. It also symbolizes values.

If you have a wide variety of wants, but a limited amount of resources with which to satisfy them, you must make value choices. Some wants are material, such as the desire for cars, houses, food, and clothing; some are mental, such as love, friendship, and power. Most, however, are combinations wherein the material want symbolizes a mental need. For example, we may want a car, but the car may actually represent a desire to be accepted or to be thought of as powerful. Thus, we want to buy a car that satisfies our ideas of social status. Although a public bus or a bicycle may satisfy the need for transportation, most life choices are not that simple. We all want to have some kind of social status, of a type determined by our value systems. In one group, a bicycle may provide that satisfaction. In another, a sports car is required. In both cases the vehicle symbolizes needs that may be more social and emotional than material.

All societies have value systems, and the people of each society share that value system in one way or another. Although some individuals and groups may reject parts or all of a society's values, the main values are largely supported in a society, or the

Table 4.1. Most Popular Magazines, 1973

| Magazine | Paid Circulation (6 month period) |
|---|---|
| TV Guide | 18,774,848 |
| Readers' Digest | 18,581,067 |
| Woman's Day | 8,234,693 |
| Family Circle | 8,187,718 |
| National Geographic | 8,185,620 |
| McCalls | 7,508,893 |
| Better Homes & Gardens | 7,979,137 |
| Ladies Home Journal | 7,026,838 |
| Playboy | 6,669,911 |
| Good Housekeeping | 5,747,368 |
| Redbook | 4,850,829 |
| American Home | 3,448,564 |
| Penthouse | 3,132,561 |

Adapted from *1974 Information Please Almanac*, Dan Golenpaul Associates, 1973. Cited source: Audit Bureau of Circulations: Publishers Statements.

value system is changed. Some general indicators of popular values can be found by observing:

1. How a society allocates its money.
2. What kinds of positions have popular status.
3. What do people do with their time and money.
4. Which media reach the most people.
5. Other factors like recreation, family living style, reading habits, clothing, furniture, music tastes, and related popular activities.

Not all of these will be examined in this book. Instead, we will examine samples of available data on some of these indicators.

The federal budget reveals much about our value system. An examination of how the United States allocates its money provides a view of those things valued in the country and promoted by its pressure groups.

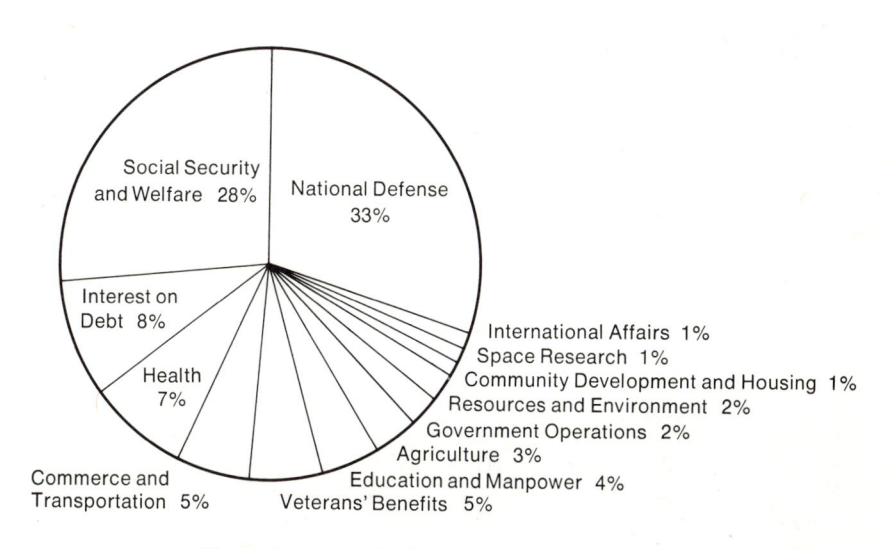

**Figure 4.1.   United States Budget Expenses**

- Social Security and Welfare 28%
- National Defense 33%
- Interest on Debt 8%
- Health 7%
- Commerce and Transportation 5%
- Veterans' Benefits 5%
- Education and Manpower 4%
- Agriculture 3%
- Government Operations 2%
- Resources and Environment 2%
- International Affairs 1%
- Space Research 1%
- Community Development and Housing 1%

Table 4.1 shows which magazines had the largest reported circulations during a six-month period in 1973. These data indicate the level of popularity of some kinds of magazines and

## 50  Values and Society

suggest one avenue for observing American values in mass media. What do they have in common? What differences exist? What values are expressed?

A Gallup Poll of the views of youth in several countries was reported in 1973. One of the questions dealt with the way youth usually spend their time on weekends. The activities identified as most and least usual in seven countries are shown in Table 4.2.

### Table 4.2. Spending Time on Weekends

| Activities | Brazil | India | Japan | Philippines | Sweden | U.S. | Yugoslavia |
|---|---|---|---|---|---|---|---|
| *Most usual* (highest 5 % reported) | | | | | | | |
| Watch TV, read magazines | 43 | | 56 | | 49 | 46 | 53 |
| Join friends | 33 | 55 | | 45 | 73 | 71 | 60 |
| Read, listen to music | 41 | 52 | 32 | 50 | 51 | 54 | 61 |
| Shop | | | 36 | | | | |
| Movies, sports events | 44 | 55 | | 33 | 51 | 60 | 58 |
| Picnics, short trips | | | 30 | | 42 | | |
| Work around house | | 55 | 29 | 69 | 42 | 53 | 48 |
| Study or work | 30 | 45 | | | | | |
| Go to church | | | | 65 | | | |
| *Least usual* (lowest 3 % reported) | | | | | | | |
| Idleness | | | | 9 | 10 | | 11 |
| Play musical instrument | 6 | 6 | | | | 14 | |
| Garden, hobby work | 5 | | 5 | | | | |
| Take walks | | | | | | 25 | |
| Picnics, short trips | | 11 | | 10 | | | |
| Go to church | | 1 | | | 6 | | |
| Volunteer work | 3 | 11 | 3 | 10 | 6 | 9 | 11 |

Adapted from: *Gallup Poll Index,* Report No. 100, Princeton, October 1973.

Figure 4.2 shows the percentage of households in the United States that owned cars and certain major appliances (according to income level).

Can you say anything about values from looking at the tables and figures in this chapter? Is there any consistency in values expressed? What other information would be needed to

Values and Social Institutions 51

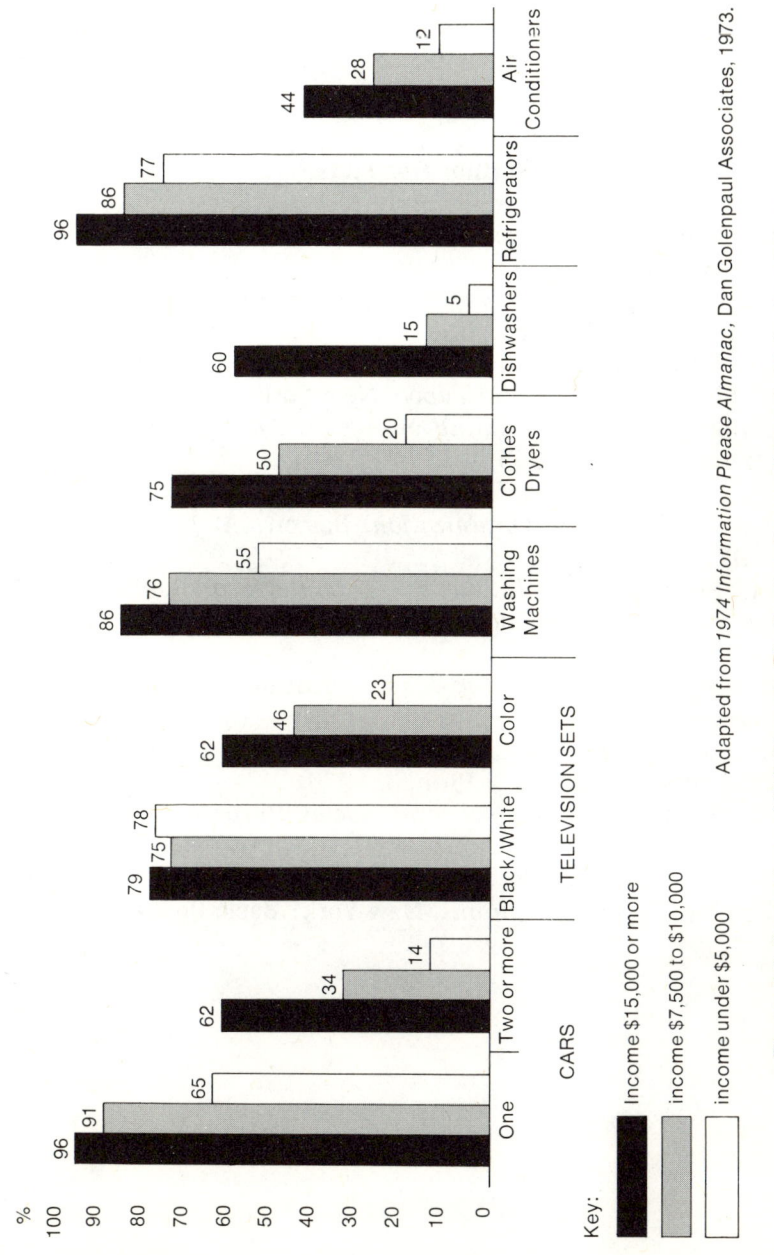

**Figure 4.2. Percentage of U.S. Households Owning Cars and Certain Major Appliances According to Income Levels.**

Key:
- ■ Income $15,000 or more
- ▨ Income $7,500 to $10,000
- □ Income under $5,000

CARS:
- One: 96, 91, 65
- Two or more: 62, 34, 14

TELEVISION SETS:
- Black/White: 79, 75, 78
- Color: 62, 46, 23

Washing Machines: 86, 76, 55
Clothes Dryers: 75, 50, 20
Dishwashers: 60, 15, 5
Refrigerators: 96, 86, 77
Air Conditioners: 44, 28, 12

Adapted from *1974 Information Please Almanac*, Dan Golenpaul Associates, 1973.

examine social values? How do your personal values compare with those suggested?

Social institutions, like language, convey social values. Identify examples of social institutions in your own area. What are the ways these examples use to express values? What are the values expressed?

### Further Readings

Berger, Peter and Brigitte. *Sociology*. New York: Basic Books, 1972.
Cummings, Elaine. *Systems of Social Regulation*. New York: Atherton Press, 1968.
Dewey, John. *Freedom and Culture*. New York: Putnam, 1939.
Freud, Sigmund. *Totem and Taboo*. New York: Norton, 1950.
Friedenberg, Edgar Z. *Coming of Age in America*. New York: Random House, 1965.
Harris, C. C. *The Family*. New York: Praeger, 1969.
Hughes, Helen. *Social Organization*. Boston: Allyn and Bacon, 1971.
Lipset, Seymour. *Revolution and Counterrevolution: Change and Persistence in Social Structure*. New York: Basic Books, 1968.
Lynd, Robert. *Knowledge for What?* Princeton: Princeton University Press, 1939.
Nelson, Jack, and Besag, Frank. *Sociological Perspectives in Education*. New York: Pitman, 1970.
Simey, T. S. *Social Science and Social Purpose*. New York: Shocken Books, 1968.
Wakeford, John. *The Cloistered Elite*. New York: Praeger, 1969.
Wells, Alan. *Social Institutions*. New York: Basic Books, 1970.

# Chapter 5

# An American Tradition

One source of values and value conflicts is the cultural tradition of a society. Several different cultures are briefly discussed in this text. What about the cultural tradition of people living in the United States? While we are not a totally separate culture from Canada, South America, and Europe, we have some national values that are somewhat different from those of our cultural relations. Americans share a common western culture that includes similarities in language, religion, customs, and beliefs. Ideas about the nature of man, his relation to other parts of his environment, and his relation to the unknown are parts of what is called the western cultural heritage.

A belief in man's rationality, his ability to exert control over his environment, and his acceptance of a single diety are within this tradition. This is the Judeo-Christian ethic that has dominated western thought even though many minority groups do not agree with it. The United States is primarily the historical product of Western Europe and continues to be heavily influenced by values brought by early settlers and later immigrants from that region of the world. Certainly, there has been variation and change over time, and of course American ideas have also greatly influenced other parts of the world; but we remain culturally related to Western Europe, as do Canada and most of South America.

### Unity, Diversity, and Individuality

Obviously, some strong subcultural differences exist within this western cultural value network. Ethnic groups now in the

United States often retain ties to nonwestern cultures, although they typically adopt western manners of dress and speech. For example, many Asians living in communities in New York, San Francisco, and other locations continue religious, family, and personal practices from their homelands in preference to western-style practices. Other groups, western or nonwestern, also prefer to engage in activities that reflect their national, religious, or racial origins. Celebrations of the Chinese New Year, Jewish holidays, Greek Name Days, and the German Oktoberfest are examples. Within this cultural diversity, often described as pluralism, lies one of our value controversies.

Mass movements in America have protested the idea of pluralism because, they contend, it weakens the unity of the mass by focusing on groups. Attempts to develop a mass ideological movement toward socialism have been frustrated because various subgroups have differing ideas of how it should function. Irish and Italian workers may disagree with Chinese and Japanese workers over some values, but agree on some union values. Black, red, white, and yellow people may disagree on how integration should occur, if at all, and may thus weaken mass movements toward a unified society.

Conversely, values that support the idea of individual liberty often see cultural pluralism as group conformity. They argue that identification with a racial, national, religious, or other ethnic group denies the independence of the individual, and makes government subject to group pressures and special interests rather than individual needs.

These issues can be considered under three categories: unity, diversity, and individuality. Unity suggests that what benefits the total society benefits each group and each person; diversity promotes the idea that subgroup cohesion and competition improve living for all people; and individuality argues that when each person has liberty, all people have it. While these goals sound comfortably similar and familiar, they have provoked wide dispute as value positions, and are the basis for a long history of tension in the United States.

### Migration and Restriction

During Colonial America, settlement by various European nations was often accompanied by restrictions against the people of other nations. The Spanish controlled their new-world settlements, limited the number of Spaniards who could move there, and permitted only native-born Spaniards and Roman Catholics to settle. Native American Indians were required to work on Spanish colonial estates and in the mines. The Spaniards felt that this narrow contact with the Spanish civilization, along with some intermarriage between Spanish soldiers and Indian women, would help civilize (or change the values of) the Indians.

The French, settling New France along the St. Lawrence and Mississippi Rivers and around the Great Lakes, also limited settlement to those of the Roman Catholic faith, and attempted to convert Indians to Christianity. The English colonies were not as restrictive, although they apparently often treated the Indians more brutally than did the French or Spanish.

The European colonizers were generally intolerant of ethnic diversity. The Massachusetts Bay Colony, settled mainly by English Puritans, exemplifies this strong feeling of unified beliefs and values that mark one kind of American tradition. The Puritans were convinced that they had the true faith and that permitting different religious views would damage their own purity. Church attendance was made compulsory. Everyone was taxed to support the church. Non-Puritans were prohibited from holding public office. And everyone was expected to live by strict Puritan rules of conduct.

This cultural tradition of dual belief in encouraging yet restricting immigrants to the United States reveals some ambivalent values of this society. The differing values of diversity versus unity; openness versus restrictiveness, and ethnic tolerance versus ethnic discrimination have plagued decision-making in the United States since its beginnings.

George Washington stated in 1783: "The bosom of America is open to receive not only the opulent and respectable stranger, but the oppressed and persecuted of all nations and religions; whom we shall welcome to a participation of all our rights and privileges if, by decency and propriety of conduct, they appear to merit the enjoyment."

Notice that Washington included a significant "if" clause that limited participation to those of "decency and propriety of conduct." These are value judgments, though the main thrust of Washington's statement is toward openness to immigrants. This sentiment is echoed in a poem by Emma Lazarus that is inscribed at the base of the Statue of Liberty:

> ". . . Give me your tired, your poor,
> Your huddled masses yearning to breathe free,

The wretched refuse of your teeming shore.
Send these, the homeless, tempest-tost, to me,
I lift my lamp beside the golden door!

These values contrast sharply with those contained in other United States actions. The Alien and Sedition Acts of 1798 were passed as a result of national hysteria that French, English, and Irish immigrants were likely to be pro-French at a time when America was on the verge of war with the French republic. The fear of immigrants led to a series of laws that included extending the naturalization period for citizenship from 5 to 14 years, and giving the President power to deport any foreign-born person considered to be a threat to the United States. The Sedition Act provided that anyone who spoke or wrote anything "false, scandalous, or malicious" about the United States Congress or the President in order to hold them in ridicule or to provoke resistance to American laws could be arrested, fined, and imprisoned.

Public controversy surrounding the Alien and Sedition Acts prevented its effective enforcement and most of its limits expired in 1800. Nevertheless, strong criticism of open immigration continued. The original citizenship law, enacted in 1970, allowed naturalization for "free, white persons," a move meant to separate and exclude slaves and blacks. It was altered after the Civil War to permit persons of "African descent" to become citizens, but not the many Chinese workers on the West Coast.

During and after the late 1800s, a series of world events created a rush of immigrants to America, threatening the values of many descendants of earlier immigrations. Workers from Italy, Greece, and Austria-Hungary came to escape poverty; and Jews from Russia, Latvia, and Lithuania came to escape religious persecution. These and others in the wave of "new" immigrants found less open space than had earlier immigrants to the United States. As a result, they tended to cluster by nationality in cities, to continue religious and language identities, and to develop ghetto-like neighborhoods. Even though earlier settlers had done virtually the same thing, America's social system had by now changed, and the new groups were seen by some as a challenge to the value of unity. One of the results was increased pressure to restrict immigration according to racial and national origins. By the 1920s this pressure had produced immigration laws based on national origin quotas. These persisted for 39 years. In 1965 changes in the laws eliminated national origins as the basis and substituted general limits by world regions and selected family or job qualifications as the criteria for admission.

Table 5.1 shows the officially recognized number of immigrants to the United States during various years between 1820 to 1950. It does not show all countries, nor does it indicate the numbers of persons who were imported as slaves or those who obtained entry without official approval.

The extreme right column shows the total number of immigrants for each year. The peak year (not shown) was 1907, when 1,285,349 immigrants arrived. From 1903, with about 850,000 immigrants, through 1914, when over 1,218,000 came, almost 12 million people moved to the United States from other areas of the world, an average of about one million per year. Comparatively, from 1933 to 1944 there were only 525,000 immigrants, an average of 43,750 per year. The only comparable 12-year period between 1820 and 1950 was from 1820 to 1831, when about 175,000 left their homes to settle in the United States.

Western European countries have provided the predominant number of immigrants. This pattern has held except during World Wars I and II, when more persons came from Canada, Mexico, and the other Americas than from Europe. Periods of war, economic instability, and restrictive legislation seem to be the main influences accounting for fluctuations in immigration. What might other factors be? What regions of the world are least represented in these immigration data? Why?

Table 5.2 shows the population of the United States in 1971 according to selected identifiable races, ethnic origins, and sex. (While there is some argument about whether distinct races actually exist or whether we are all variations in one race, the government classifies population data this way.) As the table indicates, there is little difference between numbers by sex, but considerable differences in ethnic origin. Do you think the ethnic groups shown have differing values? What value conflicts might be expected from this mixture of peoples? What value changes might occur as a result of changes in the mixtures shown? Would values alter with a change in the near balance of sexes?

### American Languages

To further underscore the complexities of unity, diversity, or individuality, Table 5.3 shows the great variety of languages spoken as mother tongues by people in the United States.

Table 5.1. Immigration to United States, by Selected Countries, 1820–1950

| | Asia Japan | China | Others | Africa Total | Americas Canada | Mexico | Others | Europe Gr. Brit. | Germany | Italy | Others | Other Areas | Total |
|---|---|---|---|---|---|---|---|---|---|---|---|---|---|
| 1820 | 0 | 1 | 4 | 1 | 209 | 1 | 177 | 2,410 | 968 | 30 | 4,283 | 301 | 8,385 |
| 1850 | 0 | 3 | 4 | 0 | 9,376 | 597 | 5,795 | 51,085 | 78,896 | 431 | 177,911 | 45,822 | 369,980 |
| 1895 | 3 | 16,437 | 59 | 54 | 24,097 | 610 | 1,933 | 47,905 | 47,769 | 3,631 | 83,656 | 2,612 | 228,770 |
| 1900 | 12,635 | 1,247 | 4,064 | 30 | 396 | 237 | 4,822 | 12,509 | 18,507 | 100,135 | 293,549 | 441 | 448,572 |
| 1910 | 2,720 | 1,968 | 18,845 | 1,072 | 56,555 | 18,691 | 14,288 | 68,941 | 31,283 | 215,537 | 610,530 | 1,140 | 1,041,570 |
| 1920 | 9,432 | 2,330 | 5,743 | 648 | 90,025 | 52,361 | 20,280 | 38,471 | 1,001 | 95,145 | 111,678 | 2,887 | 430,001 |
| 1930 | 837 | 1,589 | 2,109 | 572 | 65,254 | 12,703 | 10,147 | 31,015 | 26,569 | 22,327 | 67,527 | 1,051 | 241,700 |
| 1940 | 102 | 643 | 1,168 | 202 | 11,078 | 2,313 | 4,431 | 6,158 | 21,520 | 5,302 | 17,474 | 365 | 70,756 |
| 1950 | 100 | 1,280 | 2,399 | 849 | 21,885 | 6,744 | 15,562 | 12,755 | 128,592 | 12,454 | 45,314 | 1,253 | 249,187 |

Adapted from *Historical Statistics of the United States*, U.S. Department of Commerce, Bureau of the Census, Washington, D.C., 1960.

**Table 5.2. U.S. Population: Race, Ethnic Origin, and Sex**

(Numbers in Thousands)

| Race | Total | (%) | Male | (%) | Female | (%) |
|---|---|---|---|---|---|---|
| White | 177,626 | (87.6) | 86,420 | (87.8) | 91,206 | (87.3) |
| Black | 22,810 | (11.2) | 10,795 | (11.0) | 12,015 | (11.5) |
| Others | 2,412 | ( 1.2) | 1,205 | ( 1.2) | 1,207 | ( 1.2) |
| *European Origin* | | | | | | |
| English, Scotch, Welsh | 31,006 | (15.3) | 14,852 | (15.2) | 16,154 | (15.5) |
| French | 5,189 | ( 2.6) | 2,509 | ( 2.5) | 2,679 | ( 2.6) |
| German | 25,661 | (12.7) | 12,854 | (13.1) | 12,806 | (12.3) |
| Irish | 16,325 | ( 8.0) | 7,706 | ( 7.8) | 8,619 | ( 8.3) |
| Italian | 8,744 | ( 4.3) | 4,351 | ( 4.4) | 4,381 | ( 4.2) |
| Polish | 4,941 | ( 2.4) | 2,444 | ( 2.5) | 2,497 | ( 2.4) |
| Russian | 2,132 | ( 1.1) | 1,038 | ( 1.1) | 1,094 | ( 1.0) |
| *Spanish Origin* | | | | | | |
| Central or South American | 501 | ( 0.2) | 235 | ( 0.2) | 267 | ( 0.3) |
| Cuban | 626 | ( 0.3) | 313 | ( 0.3) | 313 | ( 0.3) |
| Mexican | 5,023 | ( 2.5) | 2,562 | ( 2.6) | 2,461 | ( 2.4) |
| Puerto Rican | 1,450 | ( 0.7) | 655 | ( 0.7) | 795 | ( 0.7) |
| Other Spanish | 1,356 | ( 0.7) | 654 | ( 0.7) | 703 | ( 0.7) |
| Others not on list | 99,905 | (49.2) | 48,248 | (49. ) | 51,658 | (49.5) |
| Totals | 202,848 | | 98,420 | | 104,428 | |

Adapted from Current Population Reports, No. 224, U.S. Department of Commerce, Bureau of the Census, October 1971.

Presumably, one way to develop unity is through a common means of communication. As Table 5.3 indicates, English is the most common language, a mark of unity in one sense, but one that effectively puts non-English speakers at a disadvantage. By emphasizing one language, linguistic diversity is discouraged. Individuality in language, however, would create havoc in any society. Imagine trying to conduct a country's business, operate its transportation systems, organize its knowledge, or meet its emergencies without a common tongue.

Noah Webster argued in 1789 the need for a national language for Americans. He saw the development of the "American tongue" as appropriate for a new nation, and as a way of cleaning up the faults of English pronunciation. For example, he wanted to eliminate all superfluous or silent letters such as ". . . *a* in bread. Thus, bread, head, give, breast, built, meant,

## Table 5.3. Languages Spoken in the United States

| | No. of People | | No. of People |
|---|---|---|---|
| English | 160,717,113 | Iraqi | 2,413 |
| Celtic | 88,162 | Near Eastern Arabic | |
| Norwegian | 612,862 | dialects | 66,064 |
| Swedish | 626,102 | | |
| Danish | 194,462 | North African Arabic | |
| Dutch | 350,748 | dialects | 408 |
| Flemish | 61,889 | Southern Semitic | 1,354 |
| French | 2,598,408 | Hamitic | 948 |
| Breton | 32,722 | Swahili | 3,991 |
| | | Libyan | 410 |
| German | 6,093,054 | Niger-Congo (Chari-Nile) | 6,537 |
| Polish | 2,437,938 | Eastern Sudanic | 2,543 |
| Czech | 452,812 | | |
| Slovak | 510,366 | Turkish | 24,123 |
| Hungarian | 447,497 | Other Uralic | 15,191 |
| Serbo-Croatian | 239,455 | Altaic | 974 |
| Slovenian | 82,321 | Hindi (Hindustani) | 26,253 |
| Dalmatian | 9,802 | Other Indo-Aryan | 22,939 |
| Albanian | 17,382 | | |
| | | Dravidian | 8,983 |
| Finnish | 214,168 | Korean | 53,528 |
| Lithuanian | 292,820 | Japanese | 408,504 |
| Other Balto-Slavonic | | Chinese (n.e.c.) | 337,283 |
| dialects | 19,748 | Mandarin | 1,697 |
| Russian | 334,615 | Cantonese | 5,819 |
| Ukrainian | 249,351 | Other Chinese dialects | 632 |
| Georgian | 757 | | |
| Rumanian | 56,590 | Tibetan | 352 |
| Yiddish | 1,593,993 | Burmese | 1,581 |
| Gypsy (Romani) | 1,588 | Thai (Siamese), Lao | 14,416 |
| | | Malay (Indonesian) | 6,253 |
| Greek | 458,699 | Other Malayan | 4,042 |
| Italian | 4,144,315 | Tagalog | 217,907 |
| Spanish | 7,823,583 | Polynesian | 20,687 |
| Portuguese | 365,300 | | |
| Basque | 8,108 | Algonquin | 19,909 |
| | | Navajo | 91,860 |
| Armenian | 100,495 | Other Athapaskan | 18,528 |
| Persian | 20,553 | Uto-Aztecan | 245 |
| Other Persian dialects | 3,370 | Other American Indian | 137,663 |
| Hebrew | 101,686 | All other | 880,779 |
| Arabic (n.e.c.) | 123,744 | Not reported | 9,317,873 |
| Egyptian | 891 | Total | 203,210,158 |

Source: *Census of Population: National Origin and Language,* U.S. Department of Commerce, Bureau of the Census, Washington, D.C., June 1973.

realm, friend, would be spelt bred, hed, giv, brest, bilt, ment, relm, frend." Webster believed that a uniform language would have several advantages, namely:

1. Foreigners would be able to pronounce it without so much difficulty.
2. Persons of all ranks would speak and write the same and this would "remove prejudice and conciliate mutual affection and respect."
3. Books would be shorter by one-eighteenth and that would save expense.
4. Most important, it would make an obvious difference between English words and American; ". . . a national language is a band of a national union."

A number of values are suggested in Webster's position, preeminently that unity is of importance. But a more current view is that diversity of language has value in a society which draws from diverse cultures. The United States has a long history of immigration, and with the mixture of peoples came a rich mixture of languages. Table 5.3 illustrates this variety as well as the commonality.

### Minorities and Unity

Historically, there have been four approaches to the treatment of minorities in American life:

1. The melting-pot concept, in which ethnic groups merge to become a new society.
2. Assimilation of Anglo-American values, attitudes, and behaviors.
3. Cultural pluralism to preserve cultural identity within a federation.
4. Separation into segregated groups.

### The Melting-Pot and Assimilation

The basic idea of the melting-pot is one of unity. The use of the term *melting-pot* is symbolic of the way metal alloys are made. Separate, more or less pure, strains of basic metals are melted together to produce a new metal which combines the best parts of each of the base metals. St. John de Crèvecoeur, an American of French descent, said in 1782 that, "Here individuals of all nations are melted into a new race of men, whose labours and posterity will one day cause great changes in the world." What this new race, this American, would be was not certain, but early predictions were mainly positive.

The melting-pot notion has had a number of supporters, and Chapter 7 examines supposed American characteristics, but it is indeed difficult to differentiate Americans as a distinct race.

The melting-pot theory and assimilation both assume a strong central unity. Melting-pot approaches consider the new society as its own unity with no necessary links to ancestor-societies. Assimilation approaches assume that one social tradition is superior and that others should therefore adapt to it. Assimilation of Anglo-American ideas by immigrants from other traditions has been the most typical form of approach to national unity in the United States. Even the native American Indians have been expected to adopt Anglo-American ways of life and thought.

Indians, still carrying a name resulting from Columbus' navigational error, were the first Americans and had thriving cultures among many organized groups before they were "discovered." American Indians are unique among minority groups. Their immigration into what is now known as the United States predated all European immigrants by more than 12,000 years, and they are the only group to have had official recognition as a nation within the United States by the U.S. Government.

That recognition, which ended in 1871, was for negotiation purposes and had little to do with prevailing ideas for forging a unity by assimilation. Indians were treated as uncivilized barbarians; their lands were taken from them; they were the last group to be granted U.S. citizenship; once they were penned up in reservations while decisions were made on how they could be assimilated into the Anglo-American mainstream. This was not a melting-pot concept; here the idea was to cause the Indians to abandon their own cultural values and to absorb the values of the dominant white society.

In addition to restricting immigration as a way of resolving value conflicts in America, laws and education have played a continuing part in forging a unity among diverse groups.

From the period of the United States Revolution to the mid-twentieth century, there has been a strong belief in the idea that immigrant groups could be brought into the mainstream of American life. This is the concept of assimilation—the idea that separate subcultures will lose their unique identities and become a single unity known as "Americans." This became a dominant value and was the reason behind a number of laws regulating subcultural practices that ran counter to mainstream beliefs. Such laws included a prohibition against the Mormon practice of multiple wives. Compulsory education was partly to ensure that immigrant children learned "the American ways." The English language was and is taught to all children in school, and American flag salutes and other patriotic exercises are standard practice in American schools. Courses in United States history and government are often required by state laws. Requirements for citizenship for those not born in the United States or having American parents include learning English and having some knowledge of United States history and government.

Benjamin Franklin, in a letter to Peter Collinson in 1753, made the following comments on "civilizing" the Indians and the German immigrants by getting them to learn English ways:

> The proneness of human nature to a life of ease, of freedom from care and labor, appears strongly in the little success that has hitherto attended every attempt to civilize our American Indians. In their present way of living, almost all their wants are supplied by the productions of nature, with the addition of very little labor, if hunting and fishing may indeed be called labor, where game is so plenty. They visit us frequently, and see the advantages that arts, sciences, and compact societies procure us. They are not deficient in natural understanding; and yet they have never shown any inclination to change their manners of life for ours, or to learn any of our arts. . . . When white persons, of either sex, have been taken prisoners by the Indians, and lived awhile with them, though ransomed by their friends, and treated with all imaginable tenderness to prevail with them to stay among the English, yet in a short time they become disgusted with our manner of life, and the care and pains that are necessary to support it, and take the first opportunity of escaping again into the woods, from whence there is no redeeming them.

Franklin goes on to describe, with some chagrin, what happened after a treaty between Indians and colonists when the English offered to take "half a dozen of their [the Indians'] brightest lads and bring them up in the best manner." The English proposed to educate these Indians in a college where they would learn languages, arts, and sciences. The Indians discussed the proposal and, recalling the effects of education on some earlier Indians educated at that same college, responded that, "for a long time after they returned to their friends, they were absolutely good for nothing; being neither acquainted with the true methods of killing deer, catching beavers, or surprising an enemy." Franklin continues that the Indians counteroffered to have the English send a dozen or two of their children to Onondago where "the Great Council would take care of their education, bring them up in what was really the best manner, and make men of them."

In over two hundred years of intervening time have values changed? Which do you think was the better education? What criteria do you use in making this judgment?

Franklin's letter about the Indians also contains comments about the threat of German immigrants to British life in the colonies. He remarks that "Those [Germans] who come hither are generally the most stupid of their own nation, and, as ignorance is often attended with credulity when Knavery would mislead it, and with suspicion when honesty would set it right; and as few of the English understand the German language, . . . it is almost impossible to remove any prejudices they may entertain." Franklin argues that German immigration should be channeled to other colonies before they outnumber the English and cause the loss of English customs, language, and government.

Thomas Jefferson, in a letter written in 1785, showed the same national prejudices that Franklin had suggested three decades earlier, but Jefferson wrote as a citizen of the new United States in describing the advantages of an American education over a European one. While wealthy people considered European college superior, Jefferson observed:

> Let us view the disadvantages of sending a youth to Europe. To enumerate them all would require a volume. I will select a few. If he goes to England, he learns drinking, horse racing and boxing. . . . He acquires a fondness for European luxury and dissipation and a contempt for the simplicity of his own country; he is fascinated with the privileges of the European aristocrats, and sees with abhorence the lovely equality which the poor enjoy with the rich in his own country; . . . He is led by the strongest of human passions into a spirit of female intrigue . . . or a passion for whores, destructive of his health, and, in both cases, learns to consider fidelity to the marriage bed as an

ungentlemanly practice. . . . He returns to his own country a foreigner, unacquainted with the practices of domestic economy necessary to preserve him from ruin, speaking and writing his native tongue as a foreigner. . . .

In this one excerpt are a variety of value judgments about England, education, youth, and, by implication, American value standards. Presumably, if the same youth went to a college in the United States he would *not* learn drinking, horse racing, boxing, dissipation, aristocratic privilege, unhealthy sex, infidelity, poor business practices, or inadequate language skills. Almost 200 years later, the status of the values Jefferson described for American colleges is still not certain.

What Webster, Franklin, Jefferson, and others were promoting was a unity concept of American society in which the ideals of liberty, justice, and equality could be attained. Commonness of language and social institutions were seen as means for pulling together peoples of scattered origins. Symbols and rituals, designed to stimulate belief in the "United" aspect of the United States, were developed and extolled. The flag, the Pledge of Allegiance, and the national anthem are examples. The Great Seal of the United States of America, adopted in 1782, contains several references to unity.

The eagle was a symbol of victory and power in Europe, and was used by native American Indians also. The shield, unsupported to signify self-reliance, has thirteen red and white stripes for the original states, bound together in the upper part by a blue band to denote their unity. The stars breaking through symbolize the birth of a new sovereign nation. An olive branch in one eagle talon signifies peace, while the arrows symbolize defense. The motto, *E Pluribus Unum,* expresses unity in its meaning— "one from many." On the reverse side of the seal, the pyramid signifies the solid building of a union as yet unfinished. The eye in the triangle above the pyramid base has been interpreted as the eye of providence set in the symbol for trinity. *Annuit Coeptis* means *God has favored our undertakings,* and *Novus Ordo Seciorum* is translated, *a new order of the ages.* Thus the values of unity, religion, sovereignty, and power are all symbolically represented in the seal.

### Minorities and Diversity

Not all people share the concept of American unity, or the means used to achieve it. Even Benjamin Franklin complained about the selection of the bald eagle as a symbolic national bird because, ". . . he is a bird of bad moral character; like those among men who live by sharping and robbing, he is generally poor, and often very lousy." Franklin preferred the turkey as a "much more respectable bird." His jibe, though, was at a symbol, not the concept or operation of unity. A more serious concern was, and is, the treatment of minority groups in a country made up of minorities. One of the tenets of American democracy is that the majority rules but that the minorities' rights are protected. This represents part of the tension between ideas of unity and ideas of diversity, for individual and group values often conflict with majority decisions.

Everyone in the United States is a member of some minority groups. No single national origin, religion, social club, political party, or recreational organization can claim a clear majority of all people. Yet numbers are not the only way to determine minorities. A group's status, as defined by the society or as seen by members of the group, also determines a minority's characteristics. Women, a numerical majority in American society, have minority-group status because society has limited their equality of opportunity, and members of the group have recognized that status. The inability of women to obtain certain kinds of education, jobs, and important social positions indicates minority-group status. On the other hand, white Anglo-Saxon Protestant males do not consider themselves to be a minority group, nor are they treated as such by laws and social status, even though they represent only about 20 per cent of the entire population of the United States.

Minority group, then, can be determined by numbers, or status, or both. In any case the United States is an aggregate of minority groups which share some common, and some divergent, characteristics and values. Some common elements have been suggested; what about the diversity?

Recent studies of groups in America show that the completely unified society has not been realized. Nathan Glazer and Daniel Moynihan conducted research on ethnic groups in New York City and published the results under the title, *Beyond the Melting Pot: The Negroes, Puerto Ricans, Jews, Italians, and Irish of New York City.* Basically, their research indicated that the concept of America as a melting-pot of different cultures was a myth and that America, if New York City is any sample, is actually a composite of virtually separate ethnic groups.

Other current indicators of group separateness include the Black Nationalist movement, the White Citizens Councils, and La Raza Unida Party of independent Chicanos. These and many other ethnic groups strive for recognition of, and respect for, the differences among American citizens and for a higher degree of decision-making power for their groups.

What are the differences among unity, diversity, and individuality in America? Which comes closest to your view of what should be? Is there a true set of American values?

The Bill of Rights, first ten amendments to the U.S. Constitution, and some related, more recent, amendments, contain some of the basic values of Americans:

### The Bill of Rights and Related Amendments

*Amendment I*

Congress shall make no law respecting an establishment of religion, or prohibiting the free exercise thereof; or abridging the freedom of speech, or of the press; or the right of the people peaceably to assemble, and to petition the Government for a redress of grievances.

*Amendment II*

A well regulated Militia, being necessary to the security of a free State, the right of the people to keep and bear Arms, shall not be infringed.

*Amendment III*

No Soldier shall, in time of peace be quartered in any house, without the consent of the Owner, nor in time of war, but in a manner to be prescribed by law.

*Amendment IV*

The right of the people to be secure in their persons, houses, papers, and effects, against unreasonable searches and seizures, shall not be violated, and no Warrants shall issue, but upon probable cause, supported by Oath or affirmation, and particularly describing the place to be searched, and the persons or things to be seized.

*Amendment V*

No person shall be held to answer for a capital, or otherwise infamous crime, unless on a presentment or indictment of a Grand Jury, except in cases arising in the land or naval forces, or in the Militia, when in actual service in time of War or public danger; nor shall any person be subject for the same offense to be twice put in jeopardy of life or limb; nor shall be compelled in any criminal case to be a witness against himself, nor be deprived of life, liberty, or property, without due process of law; nor shall private property be taken for public use, without just compensation.

*Amendment VI*

In all criminal prosecutions, the accused shall enjoy the right to a speedy and public trial, by an impartial jury of the State and district wherein the crime shall have been committed, which district shall have been previously ascertained by law, and to be informed of the nature and cause of the accusation: to be confronted with the witnesses against him; to have compulsory process for obtaining witnesses in his favor, and to have the Assistance of Counsel for his defence.

*Amendment VII*

In suits at common law, where the value in controversy shall exceed twenty dollars, the right of trial by jury shall be preserved, and no fact tried by a jury, shall be otherwise reexamined in any Court of the United States, than according to the rules of the common law.

*Amendment VIII*

Excessive bail shall not be required, nor excessive fines imposed, nor cruel and unusual punishments inflicted.

*Amendment IX*

The enumeration in the Constitution, of certain rights, shall not be construed to deny or disparage others retained by the people.

*Amendment X*

The powers not delegated to the United States by the Constitution, nor prohibited by it to the States, are reserved to the States respectively, or to the people.

*Amendment XIII*

*Section 1.* Neither slavery nor involuntary servitude, except as a punishment for crime whereof the party shall have been duly convicted, shall exist within the United States, or any place subject to their jurisdiction.
*Section 2.* Congress shall have power to enforce this article by appropriate legislation.

*Amendment XIV*

*Section 1.* All persons born or naturalized in the United States, and subject to the jurisdiction thereof, are citizens of the United States and of the State wherein they reside. No State shall make or enforce any law which shall abridge the privileges or immunities of citizens of the United States; nor shall any State deprive any person of life, liberty, or property, without due process of law; nor deny to any person within its jurisdiction the equal protection of the laws.
*Section 2.* Representatives shall be apportioned among the several States according to their respective numbers, counting

the whole number of persons in each State, excluding Indians not taxed. But when the right to vote at any election for the choice of electors for President and Vice-President of the United States, Representatives in Congress, the Executive and Judicial officers of a State, or the members of the Legislature thereof, is denied to any of the male inhabitants of such State, being twenty-one years of age, and citizens of the United States, or in any way abridged, except for participation in rebellion, or other crime, the basis of representation therein shall be reduced in the proportion which the number of such male citizens shall bear to the whole number of male citizens twenty-one years of age in such State.

Section 3. No person shall be a Senator or Representative in Congress, or elector of President and Vice-President, or hold any office, civil or military, under the United States, or under any State, who, having previously taken an oath, as a member of Congress, or as an officer of the United States, or as a member of any State legislature, or as an executive or judicial officer of any State, to support the Constitution of the United States, shall have engaged in insurrection or rebellion against the same, or given aid or comfort to the enemies thereof. But Congress may by a vote of two-thirds of each House, remove such disability.

Section 4. The validity of the public debt of the United States, authorized by law, including debts incurred for payment of pensions and bounties for services in suppressing insurrection or rebellion, shall not be questioned. But neither the United States nor any State shall assume or pay any debt or obligation incurred in aid of insurrection or rebellion against the United States, or any claim for the loss of emancipation of any slave; but all such debts, obligations and claims shall be held illegal and void.

Section 5. The Congress shall have power to enforce, by appropriate legislation, the provisions of this article.

*Amendment XV*

Section 1. The right of citizens of the United States to vote shall not be denied or abridged by the United States or by any State on account of race, color, or previous condition of servitude—

Section 2. The Congress shall have power to enforce this article by appropriate legislation.

*Amendment XIX*

*Section 1.* The right of citizens of the United States to vote shall not be denied or abridged by the United States or by any State on account of sex.
*Section 2.* Congress shall have power to enforce this article by appropriate legislation.

*Amendment XXIV*

*Section 1.* The right of citizens of the United States to vote in any primary or other election for President or Vice President, for electors for President or Vice President, or for Senator or Representative in Congress, shall not be denied or abridged by the United States or any State by reason of failure to pay any poll tax or other tax.
*Section 2.* The Congress shall have power to enforce this article by appropriate legislation.

What traditions can you identify in American society? What happens when our values and our behaviors seem to conflict? Who should interpret the meaning of values expressed in the Constitution and the Bill of Rights?

**Further Readings**

Bennis, Warren, et al. *The Planning of Change.* New York: Holt, Rinehart & Winston, 1969.
Cantril, Albert, and Roll, Charles. *Hopes and Fears of the American People.* New York: Universe Books, 1971.
Cohen, Hennig. *The American Culture.* Boston: Houghton Mifflin, 1968.
Commager, Henry S. *Meet the USA.* New York: Institute of International Education, 1970.
DeTocqueville, Alexis. *Democracy in America.* (Tr. by George Lawrence) New York: Doubleday, Anchor Books, 1969.
Dewey, John. *The Living Thoughts of Thomas Jefferson.* New York: David McKay, 1949.
Fellows, Donald K. *A Mosiac of America's Ethnic Minorities.* New York: Wiley, 1972.
Handlin, Oscar. *The Uprooted.* Boston: Little, Brown, 1973.
Harris, Jonathan. *Scientists in the Shaping of America.* Reading, Mass.: Addison-Wesley, 1971.

Hsu, Francis. *Minorities in American Life.* Belmont, Calif.: Wadsworth, 1971.
Kammen, Michael. *The Contrapuntal Civilization.* New York: Thomas Y. Crowell Co., 1971.
Kaplan, Abraham. *American Ethics and Public Policy.* New York: Oxford University Press, 1963.
Lewis, Oscar. *Children of Sanchez.* New York: Random House, 1961.
Lieberman, Jethro. *Are Americans Extinct?* New York: Walker & Co., 1968.
*Makers of America,* Vol. 1–10. Encyclopedia Britannica, 1971.
Myrdal, Gunnar. *An American Dilemma.* New York: Harper & Row, 1944.
*National Priorities.* Washington, D.C.: Public Affairs Press, 1969.
Novak, Michael. *The Rise of the Unmeltable Ethnics.* New York: Macmillan, 1972.
Roswenc, Edwin, and Bauer, F. *Liberty and Power in the Making of the Constitution.* Boston: D.C. Heath, 1963.
Shapiro, Leonard. *Totalitarianism.* New York: Praeger, 1972.
Turner, Frederick J. *The Frontier in American History.* Henry Holt & Co., 1920.

Chapter 6

# Different Cultures and Different Values

### The Cultural Filter

Language and social organization differ among various cultures of the world, and provide a way of examining differing value systems. The communications systems and social institutions which transmit values operate within a cultural tradition that carries a set of principles of human conduct, or values, into every aspect of our lives. We are born and brought up in an ongoing culture that already has a history of value choices and a number of ways of expressing them. We each carry this cultural baggage, representing a long series of social decisions about what is good and bad, right and wrong.

It is impossible for every person to learn all the knowledge of a society through learning all of the language. Organized social life permits members of a society to share in cultural traditions without extensive language information on each aspect. Such social institutions as the family, religion, government, work groups, play groups, media, and education systems transmit parts of the total cultural heritage; and their roles seemingly increase as societies become more complex. In small societies the child learns cultural traditions from the immediate family, with some knowledge gained from elders, medicine men, and certain other special social groups. In more complex societies, institutions such as schools, hospitals, prisons, law enforcement agencies, armies, newspapers, unions, and charities assume roles in the transmission of ideas and actions.

The cultural tradition provides us with a way of thinking, a means of expression and a framework for perception. This can be viewed as a maze through which we filter our experiences and select or reject ideas, sights, sounds, and values. One can think of this culture filter as a values screen through which certain information and ideas move freely, other knowledge becomes distorted, and still other concepts are deflected. Since most people have experienced only one set of cultural values, with some subcultural variations, it is difficult to consider other cultural viewpoints as legitimate. This becomes apparent to people who are able to visit areas where a strikingly different culture exists. Americans who go into the aboriginal sections of Australia or into tribal villages in parts of Africa or South America experience the result of an American culture filter. The ideas, rituals, and values of one group are confusing, unusual, and even threatening, to the outsider.

A trained anthropologist has to learn special techniques for observing different cultures to avoid making inaccurate value judgments about their life styles. This is a difficult task, perhaps even impossible. One of the controversies in anthropological study is over appropriate methods of observation. Some believe that the anthropologist should not participate in the culture being observed because it influences the level of accurate reporting in two ways: (1) the entry of an outsider changes the environment of the culture in ways that aren't always observable; and (2) by participating, the anthropologist runs the risk of adopting the values of the culture under observation, being repelled by them, or trying to change them. Others believe that it is impossible to describe a different culture accurately unless one enters into its everyday life and learns enough about the customs, taboos, and values to be able to perceive their life through their own cultural filter. One who only observes and writes notes, without experiencing the culture, develops no real understanding of why cultural behaviors exist.

Religious groups have sent missionaries to exotic areas of the world to try to convert local people to adopt the values of that religion. These missionaries have most often perceived the local culture through value filters established by the religion and as a result, their descriptions of these societies have been largely distorted.

Even before we are born the cultural tradition begins to have an impact on our lives. In a culture where science and medicine are highly valued, pregnant women are usually placed under professional medical supervision from the outset, leading up to hospitalization for childbirth. European and American societies exemplify this, although there is a movement among young people in these societies toward natural childbirth at home. Depending on one's choice of either medically supervised or natural delivery with only a midwife in attendance, a value choice has been made that will have some impact on the baby's environment.

From the moment of birth the cultural tradition of values encompasses each of us, affecting our eating habits, transportation, communication, and our thinking patterns. It has even affected our very survival. In the Greek city-state of Sparta the babies of slaves were examined to determine whether or not they were physically suited to work. Those deemed physically incapable were taken to nearby mountains to perish.

The well-known anthropologist Margaret Mead describes a somewhat different approach to infanticide in her anthropological study of the Arapesh people of New Guinea. In *The Mountain Arapesh,* Dr. Mead notes that a newborn child's sex is announced to the father. The father, from some distance away, then answers either "Wash it," or "Do not wash it." If he calls to have the child washed, the baby is saved; but if he orders that it not be washed, the baby is left to die.

Generally the value in western culture is to protect and nurture babies, although some parents neglect and abuse them. While the present cultural tradition provides for infant care, the particular cultural circumstances of the family determine the extent and type of such care. Wealthy families typically offer different infant care from poor families. Such care may not necessarily be better for the child—that itself is a value question—but the cultural disparity in wealth allows the rich different opportunities for providing for a child. The point is that the general set of values accepted in a society are the criteria against which child care is measured.

For example, the United States has developed a tradition of concern for child care and family support. If a poor family cannot adequately care for its children, special agencies, private and public, provide help. Orphanages, foster homes, adoption agencies, and welfare legislation all reflect this tradition of cultural concern, as do laws regarding child abuse. Whether it occurs in a rich or a poor family, a known case of child abuse always stirs a community's anger because such acts are opposed by the cultural value system. The rich family can afford high-priced legal assistance and may be able to keep the case from the public, but should the case become known, they run a greater risk of damage to their social standing than would a poor family.

This cultural value does not mean that a child never experiences physical punishment. Rather, the society determines what is considered acceptable violence against children and what is not. The sanctions, or social rewards and punishments, contained in laws and in areas of public arousal express which kinds of values underlie the treatment of children. In the United States parents have responsibility for their children's behavior up to a certain age. The laws, and social custom, permit parents to strike their children, so long as this form of punishment is not excessive. Parents are given much leeway in the exercise of this kind of disciplining on the grounds that it may be necessary to ensure proper behavior.

In some Japanese traditions the forced binding of a child's feet is a socially acceptable form of violence. The anger of a mother or father against a child among the Bechuana people of Africa is expressed with a mystical curse in addition to other disciplining practices. In American schools a child can be physically punished for certain antisocial behaviors. Typically, in states that permit corporal punishment, the teacher or principal administers a blow to the backside or to the hand. Many of us can remember the pinched arm, ear, or neck resulting from some infraction of a school rule. In Britain schools continue the practice of striking disobedient students with a rod across the calf of the leg or over the knuckles. In the English public boarding schools, mainly private schools for the wealthy, caning is one of the disciplinary measures used. A study reported in 1966 that over 90 percent of the public boarding schools surveyed permitted caning by school authorities.

### The Head Hunters

The Asmat people of New Guinea engage in practices that raise value questions for Americans. They have been, and presumably still are, a headhunting tribe. Headhunting was officially outlawed in the Asmat region of West Irian in 1963, but reports from visitors indicate that the practice still goes on, though not as openly. One such raid is related in a March 1972 *National Geographic* story.

The raid was undertaken to avenge an earlier killing of one Erma villager by members of a different tribe called the Pupis.

Several villages sent warriors to assist in the raid, and the women gathered and prepared food for a victory feast upon the warriors' return.

The Pupis, caught by surprise, offered little resistance. The warriors killed men, women, and children for a total of 40 dead. The bodies were taken to a place where it was believed that spirits dwelled, and the raiders dug a trench through which each body was dragged as the warriors shouted that the revenge was done and that now there could be peace. Bamboo knives were used to cut off the victims' heads and limbs, and the body parts were then brought to the Erma village. In a ceremonial house, the warriors described to the assembled people how each head had been taken. The heads were then baked and the skin removed. A hole was cut in the temple and the brains were drained and eaten. Lower jaws were taken from the heads to be worn on necklaces. The hole in the temple and removal of the lower jaw signify a head taken in a raid.

Skulls of those who died natural deaths are not cut, nor are they dismembered. Because of a belief that spirits of those killed may otherwise return, the skulls are kept in the village on display and are used as sleeping pillows to keep the ghosts away.

Despite their harsh treatment of enemies, villagers of the Asmat tribe become very emotional over the deaths of relatives. Women may roll in mud patches and cover their bodies in mud to show anguish over the death and to protect themselves from being smelled by the ghost of the deceased. Others mourn by wailing, falling to the ground, and crying loudly.

By our cultural standards, such values regarding life and death may seem peculiar or disturbing. At the same time the Asmats would likely consider modern warfare with massive bombings, napalm, and radar-controlled missiles strange and threatening. They might also view the elaborate rituals of an American-type funeral as being highly unusual.

The reason the Asmats no longer publicly engage in headhunting is that the values of the Indonesian Government, which controls this area, do not permit such activity and laws have been passed to regulate it. Since the Indonesians had the power to enforce these measures, the practice of headhunting is no longer as prominent in New Guinea. Thus, the conflict in values is partly resolved by the imposition of a stronger force. Persuasion to a different set of values is also at work in this situation, since missionaries and others have campaigned among the Asmats to get them to abandon this tradition.

Which set of values do you subscribe to? If you had grown up in a group which practiced headhunting as a ritual of strength, how do you think you would react to a different culture imposing restrictions on it? Suppose a culture of great power emerges and declares that football is too violent for people to play. What impact would that have on the American way of life? What are the cultural values involved in football, baseball, chess, and boxing? Are they related to headhunting, witch-burning, gladiators and lions, and cockfighting? What are the differences? If human life is of greater value than cultural ritual, should one society's government impose restrictions on another's? What if the values don't involve headhunting, but involve protection of the environment by modern conservation techniques? The next case raises such a question regarding cultural value change.

### The Mountain People

A recent book by anthropologist Colin Turnbull, *The Mountain People,* describes a society in northeastern Uganda that represents another example of value interaction. The people of that society are named Ik (pronounced *eek*), a group that Turnbull studied over a period of time. The Ik were moved from their original tribal grounds when the Ugandan government converted the area into a national park. Forbidden to range and hunt, the Ik were expected to adapt to farming the steep mountain slopes. The traditions and rituals that had suited them earlier as a mobile, hunting society did not fit them for sedentary life as farmers. Turnbull describes incidents among the Ik that relate to a change in social values which apparently resulted from their changed environment.

The Ik had been a peaceful society who believed that their god, Didigwari, had let each member of the tribe down from heaven on a vine and had given each a digging stick and instructions that they were not to kill people. Cooperation among tribespeople during hunts for food, and honoring the dead by ceremonies devoted to them, are typical of the group activities engaged in by the Iks before the Ugandan government began a conservation program in the Kidepo Valley where they had lived. The tribe was moved by the government to the mountainside where Turnbull spent 18 months living with them. More crowded than they had ever been before, and restricted from their normal hunting activities, the Ik developed behaviors that showed an alteration in values.

In one incident Turnbull was being led over the mountains by two Iks, who urged him to precede them through some tall grass. As Turnbull pushed his way through he nearly fell over a 1500-foot cliff. The Iks burst into laughter at the joke they had played on him. A blind woman member of the Iks had stumbled over the same cliff at another time and almost died. An entire village came to the edge of the drop and joined in laughter at the sight of the blind woman's agony.

A young child crawled toward the flames of an Ik fire as a group of tribespeople watched. When the child grabbed a hot coal and screamed with pain, the group laughed.

Youngsters laughed gaily as they came upon a weak elderly Ik. They beat him with sticks and threw stones at him until he cried.

A two-year drought had destroyed the Ik's crops and starvation had come upon the tribe just before Turnbull arrived. With a shortage of food and no opportunity to hunt in large groups as before, the Ik patterns of life and values changed from community support to individual survival, even at the sacrifice of others. A single hunter might illegally get food, but would not tell others, including his own family. He would eat as much as he could himself and blackmarket the rest to the police. The government provided food for the Ik, but the strong ones who went to the police station to get the rations for their families might stop on the way home and eat it all.

Keeping food from family and elders became a mark of distinction and the subject of stories and laughter. Old people were abandoned to die, and no honors or positive rituals were performed for them.

Colin Turnbull, writing the final paragraph in this provocative book, states:

> The Ik teach us that our much vaunted human values are not inherent in humanity at all, but are associated only with a particular form of survival called society, and that all, even society itself, are luxuries that can be dispensed with. That does not make them any the less wonderful or desirable, and if man has any greatness it is surely in his ability to maintain these values, clinging to them to an often very bitter end, even shortening an already pitifully short life rather than sacrifice his humanity. But that too involves choice, and the Ik teach us that man can lose the will to make it.

In an article in the November 1972 *Smithsonian* magazine, John B. Calhoun suggests that the Ik represent what can happen if population is permitted to grow unchecked. Calhoun had created great controversy earlier by the publication of his studies on mice which were given limited space and allowed to overpopulate it. The mice evidenced alienation, excessive aggressiveness, withdrawal, and the loss of social bonds. Calhoun proposed that this could happen to mankind in what he described as a "behavioral sink." In the *Smithsonian* article, he reviews Turnbull's book and notes the similarities between the Iks and the mouse colony. Calhoun states, "All goodness was gone from the Ik, leaving merely emptiness, valuelessness, nothingness . . ."

What values are Turnbull and Calhoun expressing? How do they differ from the values exhibited by the Ik? Are the Ik "valueless"? If you lived among the Ik do you think your values would change? Was the Ugandan government wrong in evicting the Iks to create conservation areas? Should the government stop providing famine relief because the food does not go to all of the people? Are there any similarities between the governmental treatment of the Iks and the United States government's treatment of such groups as American Indians or the Japanese living on the West Coast during World War II? Are there differences in values in these cases?

**Technology and Stone Age Man**

When differing cultural traditions meet, some kind of interchange occurs. Where the cultures are relatively close in stages of technological or economic development, it may amount to only an interchange in the refinement of special tools or techniques. For example, as the mutual reopening of Communist China and the western nations proceeds, some mutual cultural impact will doubtless occur.

Acupuncture treatments are a good example. Prior to 1972 few people in the United States knew of this Oriental approach to medical care which uses the insertion and twisting of fine steel needles in various parts of the body. If someone in Indiana had proposed such treatment for an illness in 1965, he would have been considered a quack; there was then little knowledge in the United States about this form of medical treatment, a highly developed science in Communist China. Cross-cultural visits have thus opened some intriguing new ideas for American medical science.

Business, agriculture, and the arts will also experience some cross-cultural interchange as Chinese-American exchange increases. Great differences in values exist between the two countries, and these differences may be sharpened or dulled by such international activities. Both countries, however, are relatively close in technological development. Consider the possible consequences of two cultures that vary widely, not only in values, but in stages of technology.

A small group of people known as the Tasadays live a virtual stone-age existence on the island of Mindanao in the Philippines. They were discovered by a trapper in 1966, who subsequently arranged a meeting between members of the group and Philippine officials in 1971. The news of that visit traveled widely as a result of photographers and television cameras. The Tasadays, whose technical knowledge was limited to making bamboo-bladed knives and hammers with stone heads, were confronted by men in helicopters carrying complicated equipment. To technological man the idea of scraping the pith from wild palms in order to get food, having no electricity or bathrooms, and engaging in no wars may seem incredible. Certainly the Tasadays must consider aircraft, canned food, and television cameras equally incredible. The Tasadays chose to maintain their old ways and ignore the modern marvels of science, a value choice dependent on their cultural tradition. There has, however, been some cultural interchange, for better or worse. Bows, arrows, and metal knives have been added to the Tasaday society, and stories and photos of stone-age life have been added to American society.

Which set of values do you think will be more firmly transplanted? Have stone-age values any significance for Americans today? What values underlie each culture? What additional evidence would you need to assess the values of the cultures represented in the cases in this chapter?

### Political Values in a Modern European Nation

The Swiss are considered to be among the more cosmopolitan and sophisticated of peoples, while retaining a certain old-world flavor and no imperialistic designs on other countries. With a population of a little over 6 million, Switzerland has fewer people than New York City, but the country's central location in Europe and its ability to sustain a national cohesion in spite of geographic, cultural, and language diversities make it useful as an example for consideration of national values. Switzerland, of course, is not a separate culture from Western Europe. It exemplifies a number of broader European traditions in its value system.

The Swiss descend from several ethnic groups and retain four official languages—French, German, Italian, and Romansh. Their country has rugged mountains and many lakes, but few mineral resources. It has become an international center for banking and insurance as well as skilled craftsmanship. In internal politics the country is a federal republic of 22 cantons similar to states.

In a study reported in 1973 by Armin Gretler and Pierre-Emeric Mandl, the values of the Swiss people were examined by analysis of the several political parties' statements on a variety of topics. The following is a summary of excerpts from the political parties' programs to show both common Swiss values and divergent values stressed by groups within the country.

*Conservative Christian Social People's Party (KCVP)*
. . . acknowledge the common aim of a Christian, democratic, federalistic, and social Confederation and recognize the Christian ethic as the essential foundation of both private and public life. . . . The KCVP is determined to mold public life according to Christian values . . . [we are] guided by the following universal principles: first, the social principle of individuality, which teaches that the immortal personality is the concern of creation; second, the principle of mutual support, which teaches that each person has his place in society, depends upon society and attains his purposes and goals through society; and third, the principle of subsidiarity and federalism, which proclaims that there is a right to independence and freedom within the individual sphere and that every group within the society and the nation is autonomous in that sphere and may legitimately pursue its collective well-being.

*Free Democratic Party*
The guiding factor is and remains freedom, which constitutes not just one of the various political values, but the truly fundamental value. [The Party] seeks to bring together freedom-loving fellow citizens of all occupations, classes, and faiths, of all ages and of both sexes. . . . [It] seeks the furtherance of national well-being on the basis of freedom, equality, and national sovereignty. It places the

well-being of the community above the particular interests of any section of the population, economic group, or faith.

*Social Democratic Party (SPS)*
. . . strive to attain a social order that will free human beings from economic exploitation. Irrespective of origin or property each person should be able freely to develop his character and abilities . . . Mutual support and social justice must form the pillars of human community.

*Swiss Peasants', Traders', and Citizens' Party (BGB)*
It supports all efforts directed toward preserving and strengthening our country's political autonomy and our people's spiritual independence. . . . It proclaims its belief in the ideals of the middle class. . . . It rejects any internationalism that is directed against the national community.

*Liberal Democratic Citizens' Party*
Our party is called liberal because it demands order within freedom . . . it acknowledges the essential values of Christian culture without sectarian ties. . . . It is called Democratic because it takes as its watchword: "With the people—for the people." . . . It is called a party of citizens because it proclaims the conviction that, at a time when humans are everywhere threatened by the mass, the influence of the citizen who thinks and acts as an individual must be strengthened.

*Evangelical People's Party*
God's universal domination of us humans demands that all areas of life should be subordinated to His will. . . . The Party is aiming at the development of the national community as an expression of justice, peace and mutual support.

*Labor Party (PdA)*
The theoretical basis of scientific socialism consists of dialectic materialism. Only socialist solutions can permit human development within a just and prosperous society.

Can you judge from these brief quotes what some of the common values of the Swiss people seem to be? Are they different from values you consider to be American? Do they differ from values of other cultures? What are the differences among the several parties?

84  *Values and Society*

Could you make a judgment of American values by reading the platforms of American political parties? How would you expect these values to differ from values expressed by political figures in such recently established nations in Africa as Zambia, Botswana, Gambia, or Sierra Leone?

### Subcultural Values

In addition to broad social value systems that appear to identify different cultures, there are also value systems within a culture. While group values can be considered those of a small segment of a society in one location, they can also be part of broader subcultural values. That is, group values that are important to a youth gang in one high school in Minneapolis may also be shared by similar gangs in other cities. In fact, it is highly unlikely that one is totally different from anyone or anywhere else. Group values, then, can be seen as a part of subcultural values. And *subculture* is just another way of defining a large group with common aspects.

By subculture we refer to certain characteristics, behaviors, and values of a segment of a culture which identify its members. A number of ways can be used to describe subcultures. One is to define them by national origin. Another is to define them by race or ethnic derivation. Another is by social class or occupation. Still others include age, sexual behavior, social attitudes, religions, and political views. Some examples of these breakdowns are:

| National/Ethnic Derivation | Social Class and Occupation | Age |
|---|---|---|
| Irish | Upper-class | Children |
| Puerto Ricans | Middle-class | Senior citizens |
| Africans | Working class | Youth |
| Greeks | Unemployed | Middle-aged |
| Chinese | Businessmen | Young marrieds |
|  | Students |  |

| Sexual | Religion | Political Views |
|---|---|---|
| Prudes | Fundamentalists | Hard-hats |
| Swingers | Protestants | Pacifists |
| Homosexuals | Russian Orthodox | Law and order |
| Free Lovers | Atheists | Consumer protectors |
| Feminists | Catholics | Militarists |

The top three examples are those of subculture characteristics; the bottom three are more indicative of attitudes and behaviors, although there are mixtures of these in most subcultures.

As these examples show, subcultural values are an important consideration in analyzing personal group and social values. Just as different cultures have different values, subcultures within one culture may have widely variant attitudes and beliefs.

It is relatively easy to see the differences among groups in your own society since you are a member of some subcultures and you recognize other ones. It may be more difficult to develop that same understanding of subcultures in other societies. It is also very difficult to comprehend the similarities among humans in other groups and societies when we concentrate on the differences.

A balanced view might be achieved by recognizing that in physical characteristics, personal and social behaviors, and broad values are striking similarities, and that the variety of differences attests to another commonality—that of human creativity.

Human bodies are closely similar throughout the world. The personal and social behaviors of eating, talking, walking, seeing, and touching are also dominantly common among the world's people, although they may perform them somewhat differently or derive different meanings from them. The values of justice, health, and love appear to express universal human desires, although specific definitions may differ. It is hard to believe that a group would choose such conditions as injustice, ill health, or lack of love, even though these conditions are in abundant quantities world wide.

While observing the differences among humans, it is well to reflect on the similarities. Are there human values which supercede all cultural and subcultural values?

**The United Nations and Values**

The Charter of the United Nations contains value statements agreed to by member nations. The first international declaration of human rights, it begins with the following:

WE THE PEOPLES OF THE UNITED NATIONS DETERMINED
> to save succeeding generations from the scourge of war, which twice in our lifetime has brought untold sorrow to mankind, and
> to reaffirm faith in fundamental human rights, in the dignity and worth of the human person, in the equal rights

of men and women and of nations large and small, and

to establish conditions under which justice and respect for the obligations arising from treaties and other sources of international law can be maintained, and

to promote social progress and better standards of life in larger freedom,

AND FOR THESE ENDS

to practice tolerance and live together in peace with one another as good neighbors, and

to unite our strength to maintain international peace and security, and

to ensure, by the acceptance of principles and the institution of methods, that armed force shall not be used, save in the common interest, and

to employ international machinery for the promotion of the economic and social advancement of all peoples,

HAVE RESOLVED TO COMBINE OUR EFFORTS TO ACCOMPLISH THESE AIMS.

The Universal Declaration of Human Rights was adopted by the U.N. General Assembly in 1948 without a single dissenting vote. Its thirty articles provide basic rights and freedoms for men and women everywhere without discrimination by color, sex, language, or religion. It includes freedom from slavery, and arbitrary arrest; freedom of movement, thought, expression, assembly, and association; and rights to fair trial, ownership of property, marriage, work, education, and participation in the politics and cultural life of a society. The Declaration is not a legal document, like the U.S. Constitution, but is a statement of moral, or value, principles.

It begins with the preamble:

Whereas recognition of the inherent dignity and of the equal and inalienable rights of all members of the human family is the foundation of freedom, justice and peace in the world,

Whereas disregard and contempt for human rights have resulted in barbarous acts which have outraged the conscience of mankind, and the advent of a world in which human beings shall enjoy freedom of speech and belief and freedom from fear and want has been proclaimed as the highest aspiration of the common people.

Whereas it is essential, if man is not to be compelled to have recourse, as a last resort, to rebellion against tyranny and oppression, that human rights should be protected by the rule of law,

Whereas it is essential to promote the development of friendly relations between nations,

Whereas the peoples of the United Nations have in the Charter reaffirmed their faith in fundamental human rights, in the dignity and worth of the human person and in the equal rights of men and women and have determined to promote social progress and better standards of life in larger freedom,

Whereas member states have pledged themselves to achieve, in cooperation with the United Nations, the promotion of universal respect for and observance of human rights and fundamental freedoms,

Whereas a common understanding of these rights and freedoms is of the greatest importance for the full realization of this pledge . . .

The Declaration goes on to enumerate the rights and freedoms.

What common values are expressed in these international documents? Are there societies that would not accept them? Compare these statements with the U.S. Declaration of Independence, Constitution, and Bill of Rights. Do you find apparent value differences?

Are there groups in America which would not share the values expressed in the U.N. documents? Are there groups with values they hold higher in a value hierarchy than those in the U.N. materials? Which of your personal values coincide with those of the U.N.? Which personal values conflict?

### Further Readings

*Everyman's United Nations.* New York: United Nations, 1968.
Fersh, Seymour. *Culture Regions of the World Series.* New York: Macmillan, 1970–1973.
Fraenkel, Jack, ed. *Perspectives in World Order.* New York: Random House, 1973, 1974.
Gretler, Armin, and Mandl, P. *Values, Trends and Alternatives in Swiss Society.* New York: Praeger, 1973.
Hsu, Francis. *Americans and Chinese: Two Ways of Life.* Garden City, N.Y.: Doubleday, 1972.

Kluckhohn, Clyde. *Culture and Behavior*. New York: Macmillan, 1962.
Mead, Margaret. *The Mountain Arapesh*. New York: Doubleday Natural History Press, 1968.
Morris, C. *Varieties of Human Value*. Chicago: University of Chicago Press, 1956.
Ortiz, Alfonso. *The Tewa World*. Chicago: University of Chicago Press, 1969.
Sears, R. R., Maccoby, E., and Levin, H. *Patterns of Child-Rearing*. Evanston, Ill.: Row, Peterson, 1957.
Turnbull, Colin. *The Mountain People*. New York: Simon & Schuster, 1972.

Chapter 7

# Divergent Views of the American Character

List all the main characteristics you can think of that mean American to you. After you've finished the list, compare it with the characteristics noted by others and reported here.

### The American Character

It does not take long to realize that there is nothing strikingly different about people in the United States in physical appearance. We have people of all colors, heights, weights, nose lengths, and shoe sizes, and all degrees of beauty and homeliness. It would therefore be difficult to categorize Americans as a distinct physical group. It might be possible to identify them by clothing or jewelry, but even that is clear only when native costumes of different nations are compared. Many people of other nations wear similar dress.

In behavior Americans might be more distinctive. Our use of the English language differs from that of Britain and Australia, and even to some extent from that of Canada. It is also true, however, that it differs from place to place within the United States. We eat different foods and use different utensils for cooking and eating than do a large number of other nations. We spend a lot of time in automobiles and in front of television sets in comparison with others. And we have some manners and behavior habits that are more or less distinctly American.

In the realm of ideas or beliefs, or values, what constitutes American?

From the State of Delaware Department of Public Instruction, excerpted from *The Challenge of Our Times: Democracy Faces Communism,* the following view of American values is presented:

A. *The Individual*

There is substantial individual freedom of the mind and access to a wide variety of information and points of view.

Respect for the individual is an accepted ideal.

The individual has certain rights and freedoms guaranteed by the Constitution and its amendments, such as freedom of speech and press, and is assured a fair trial.

The individual's rights and freedoms are protected by due process of law and an independent court system.

B. *Social Institutions*

Culture is the product of individuals and group thinking, acting, and creating for themselves.

The family exists for the development of the individual.

The individual is free to choose his own moral code of ethics and his own religious future.

Public education is concerned with preparing children for the making of choices.

There are various strata of society, but class differences are minimized.

C. *Economic Institutions*

The individual is free to profit from his ideas.

Competition is encouraged.

Private Enterprise is fostered.

A worker through his union may bargain collectively with his employer.

The means of production may be and generally are privately owned.

D. *Political Institutions*

Public opinion influences governmental policy; a free exchange of ideas is allowed.

Civil liberties are guaranteed by the federal constitution.

A multi-party system with opposition among and within parties is recognized.

Any qualified individual may seek office and enjoy freedom of choice by secret ballot.

Government is by the consent of the governed—of, by, and for the people.

What values are expressed and/or implied in this statement? Which would you agree are American values?

Another view of American values comes from a study of what visitors from other countries to the United States observed about Americans. This is taken from a report by William Torrence and Paul Meadows, "American Culture Themes: An Analysis of Foreign Observer Literature." The authors read what citizens of other countries said about Americans and reported the frequency that certain themes were expressed. Torrence and Meadows found the following information about American values, ranked in order based on the number of times a certain characteristic was noted:

Americans:

1. prefer individualism and prefer to be free from authority.
2. accept some superior-inferior relationship.
3. love to moralize about their interests in economic matters.
4. see the accumulation of wealth as a test of worth.
5. demand competition.
6. require standardization.
7. regard work as a moral value.
8. appreciate mechanization, organization, and efficiency.
9. enjoy practicality.
10. prefer bigness, large quantity.
11. desire comfort.
12. respect productivity.

Do you agree with this listing, and with the ranking? Do you find any value contradictions in the list?

Seymour M. Lipset, in "Constant Values in American Society," states that there are two basic values in American culture: equalitarianism and achievement. He says that the equalitarian value determines the nature of our status system, while achievement produces social mobility. Equalitarian views suggest that people are equal and should be given equal opportunities and equal treatment under the law. Thus, status is not granted by birth. Achievement emphasizes individual and group differences by focusing on abilities and rewards. In a completely equal society, doctors, fishermen, miners, and students have equal status. In an achievement society there are hierarchies according to what the society values most, and people have different social statuses.

Do these values of equality and achievement conflict? Are both American values?

Members of a committee appointed by the Florida State Superintendent of Public Instruction to develop a guide for teaching "Moral and Spiritual Values in Florida Schools" surveyed books, reports, and articles and identified the following among basic American values:

1. Man is a spiritual being of ultimate dignity and worth by virtue of the fact that he has his origin and destiny in God, his creator.
2. As a spiritual being of dignity and worth, man is to be treated as an end in himself. As a person of dignity and worth man should recognize and respect these same qualities in his fellow man.
3. As a person of dignity and worth, man should develop self-respect, and should endeavor to develop those capacities which are unique to him as an individual. He should be encouraged to preserve his unique individuality and not to become a slave to conformity.
4. All men are created equal in that they have equal worth in the sight of God, and, therefore, they have equal rights before the law and deserve equal opportunities to develop to the maximum of their innate capacities.

Are these the American values? How do they compare with the values others have described? With which values do you agree?

The McGuffey Readers, most popular of schoolbooks in Middle America during the nineteenth century, expressed moral values to generations of students based on what were considered common ideals and goals for American citizens. Presumably, the values expressed were acceptable to the society since the books were so widely used. Through stories designed to teach both reading and morality, the McGuffey Readers conveyed the values of:

1. Protestant Christianity similar to Puritanism. The Bible was to be accepted as truth, with a just but stern God, who would not hesitate to punish anyone who broke His commandments.
2. Rewards and punishments for virtue and wickedness. Honesty and thoughtfulness were richly rewarded, while disobedience and greed were punished heavily.

3. Practice in the virtues of industry, sobriety, thrift, propriety, modesty, punctuality, and conformity. Hard work, coupled with obedience and thrift, lead to success.
4. Success and failure measured in material terms. Jobs and savings represent success; failure is the result of laziness or self-indulgence.
5. Self-reliance. Individualism and independence are marks of the proper citizen. Government is not to be relied upon to provide for people's needs.

Are these values still the American Creed? What evidence do you have that learning these values changed or did not change the American character? If you were writing a story to convey American values, what would it say?

Gunnar Myrdal, the Swedish commentator on America whose book *An American Dilemma* examined the issue of race relations, describes the American Creed as the ideals of individual dignity, fundamental equality, and certain inalienable rights to freedom, justice, and fair opportunity. He says that "America is conservative in fundamental principles, but hopefully experimental in practical social arrangements." The roots of this creed, according to Myrdal, are in the idea of human rationality, belief in harmony between equal opportunity and individual liberty, faith in education, tolerance for religions, and rule by law, not men. For Blacks, as Myrdal points out, the creed is not practiced, and the dilemma of America rests in the disparity between the expressed values of equality and liberty and the unequal and oppressed status of minority groups.

Similar problems of conflicting values are expressed in *Meet the USA*, prepared by historian Henry Steele Commager for students and professors from other countries who came to America to study and teach. The book is filled with information about America, including considerations of the "American Character." Some of the characteristics and conflicts Commager notes are:

1. A belief in self-government, although there is a continuing debate over states' rights versus a strong national government.
2. Acceptance of a business civilization in which businessmen are given great power and privilege, yet a dual belief in completely free enterprise and governmental support for business and public welfare.

3. Popularity of religion with strains of emotionalism and practicality in its practice, and separation of church and state as an ideal.
4. Continuing idealization of equality while massive evidence of inequality exists.
5. Respect for laws, yet with a history of being "the most lawless nation of the western world."

Other views of American values are noted by a variety of observers:

Jean-Paul Sartre, French Existentialist, comments that in conformity Americans have great freedom. Individuals are under great pressure to conform then, since only the successful can afford to have unique personalities; the successful are permitted to regain their individuality.

Y. A. Zamoshkin, Russian writer on philosophy, suggests that the bureaucratic organization in American social life that rests upon the management efficiency needed in capitalism is destroying individualism, another American value. Thus, we come to value continuation of the bureaucracy over individual liberty.

Tom Hayden, one of the founders of Students for a Democratic Society, expressed his disenchantment with the American values of "racial bigotry," "warlike posturing," and the "supreme respect for money." He suggests that America exhibits civilized barbarism by public pretense of humanitarianism, but private satisfaction with racial inequality, exploitation of the poor, and continuation of social class separation.

Urie Bronfenbrenner, a social psychologist, studied the Soviet Union and was disturbed by what he described as a mirror-image effect in the way Russians and Americans view each other. Among the themes each nation used to perceive the other were:

1. "*They* are the aggressors." Russia is a warmonger according to the United States view, and America is a warmonger according to the Soviet opinion.
2. "*Their* government exploits and deludes the people." It is either the Communist Party which exploits or it is capitalism with its military-industrial complex.
3. "The mass of *their* people are not really sympathetic to the regime." Each believes the other would choose its opposite's form of government if the choice were open.

4. *"They* cannot be trusted." Propaganda and intrigue are national weapons of the opposite side.
5. *"Their* policy verges on madness."

In 1948 a UNESCO-supported survey was undertaken to determine various national images as perceived by people in other nations. The results of this survey showed that Europeans viewed Americans as "practical," "progressive," "generous," "hard-working," and "intelligent." Favorable adjectives *not* selected as characteristic of Americans were, "brave," "self-controlled," and "peace-loving." Negative adjectives selected to describe Americans included "conceited" and "domineering."

If such a survey were conducted today, what might be the results? Would different positive and negative adjectives be applied by Africans, Asians, or South Americans? How accurate do you think such surveys are? What adjectives would you select from the following list to describe other countries of the world? Which would you select to describe America? How do you justify your selection?

Backward          Resourceful
Materialistic     Cruel
Warmonger         Humane
Imperialistic     Domineering
Aggressive        Enterprising
Friendly          Chaotic
Racist            Civilized
Hard-working      Free
Peace-loving      Democratic
Intelligent

Which of the adjectives above do you see as positive descriptive words, and which are negative? How do you assign values to them? What are the criteria for these values?

Is it possible to characterize whole nations from a list of adjectives? Or is it a matter of drawing stereotypes from some individuals and applying them to entire countries?

### Conflicting Values

A study of five differing cultural traditions in the same region of the United States has been conducted by 30 social scientists from the fields of anthropology, sociology, psychology, philosophy, history, government, and law. The region studied was south of Gallup, New Mexico. The cultural traditions under study included small communities identified as:

Zuñi Indians
Navaho Indians
Mormons
Spanish-Americans of the Catholic religion
Texans of Protestant religions

A primary concern of the study was to examine values held by each group and the role of values in human life.

Each of the groups lives in the same general area and, presumably, sees the same plateaus and mesas, the same kinds of plant and animal life, the same sky and water, the same weather. They all experience the same changes in temperature, rainfall, wind, and storm. They walk over the same kinds of soil, breathe common air, eat food, and reproduce in the same way.

Differences occur in the ways each group tries to cope with the problems of survival and in the ways each understands the workings of society. These differences show value systems that have some similarities, some uniquenesses and some conflicts in comparison with others. None of the groups retains the "pure" culture of its ancestors. All cultures change, and these groups have had many cross-cultural contacts which have modified older traditions. Yet each has maintained a distinctive set of values and behaviors. To cope with basic human survival, the five groups have adopted some similar and some different approaches.

The Zuñi group is the oldest in this area. They long ago developed an agriculture based on irrigation. This food supply is now augmented by raising livestock. Craftwork, mainly in the form of silver jewelry, is an important economic activity among the Zuñi.

Navahos settled in this area over one hundred years ago after centuries as nomadic hunters and food gatherers. In this region they have become shepherds and farmers, depending on natural rather than irrigated water. They depend heavily for economic survival on wages earned as employees.

Wages are also important to the Spanish-Americans, who settled here about one hundred years ago. Ranching is the other dominant economic activity of this group.

The Mormons arrived here during approximately the same period as the Spanish-Americans. They have taken up irrigation farming and livestock ranching, and work for wages.

The last group to arrive was the Texans, who settled land available under the Homestead Act during the 1930s. They are cattle raisers and operate highly mechanized farming without irrigation.

In describing the value systems of each group, and judging the role that values play in maintaining cultural distinctions, anthropologists Evon Vogt and John Roberts write in *Scientific American,*

> Thus systems of values may promote and justify radically different modes of behavior among people confronted with the same objective problem.

The evidence they provide for this summary statement includes the following:

*Zuñi.* They spend winters in stone houses within a large central pueblo, but in the summer agricultural period they move to three farming villages. Their social structure is matrilocal, where the husband and wife live with the wife's family, and includes matrilineal clans, in which children are considered to be descended from the mother rather than the father. Motherhood, of course, is of great importance in such a system.

The Zuñi also have a complex, tightly structured arrangement of religious, family, and social units. Earlier Zuñis were under the rule of a theocracy, a government of religious leaders. There is a strong feeling for community authority and cooperation. A series of priesthoods, dancing groups, and curing societies serve to reinforce the positive idea of cooperation. In addition the Zuñi have large groups of relatives, or kinships, to which each member has responsibilities and from which each gets support. These obligations also foster cooperation.

The Zuñi approach to nature is also one of cooperation. They do not believe that humans have or should have control over nature. Neither do they consider humans to be mere victims of nature. Rather, their religious activities stress harmony. During periods of drought the Zuñi increase the number of ceremonies designed to appeal to the gods in the understanding that if the Zuñi do their part, the gods will respond. The Zuñi, for example, oppose artificial rainmaking.

*Navaho.* They prefer to live in hogans, six-sided log houses, scattered throughout the region. There are few village-like settlements. Like the Zuñi, they have matrilocal and matrilineal social structures, but are not organized as tightly. The Navaho tends to be more individualistic and less oriented toward community than the Zuñi. Until the middle of the twentieth century, the Navaho did not have a highly organized political system. The leadership stemmed from a loosely structured series of local Navaho groups with a common language and traditions.

A sense of kinship operates among the Navaho, but it is not as strong as that of the Zuñi. The Navaho also stress cooperation, although there are few highly structured, regular cooperative activities. At the same time, no sense of strong competition exists among the Navaho.

Navaho understandings of nature, unlike the Zuñi, is that nature is a threatening force, more powerful than humans. Fear is therefore the main emotion in their relationship with nature. Yet the Navaho believe they can, through humble rituals, maintain some harmony with nature and soften its worst threats. For the Navaho the most important time is the present, so future control of nature is not significant.

*Mormons.* They live in a closely knit village, sharing a strong sense of community. The dominant position of the Mormon religion is reflected in family and community affairs.

In this patrilocal, patrilineal group, values are perpetuated by the single church. Within its highly structured organization, however, is considerable latitude for local decisions. In addition, a strong value in the religion is that of cooperation in social and economic life.

The village maintains a variety of cooperative activities including land, cattle, and irrigation companies in the form of large family groups bound together by common religious values rather than familial ties. While kinship is important to the Mormons, it dominates only among the closest relatives.

The Mormons hold the view that nature can and should be controlled by humans. This falls within the values that humans are progressing toward Godhood, and that Mormons were put on earth to learn about and master the gross matter of their environment. The Mormons endorse new technology, including artificial rainmaking, as being consistent with these beliefs in the future and in human perfectability.

*Spanish-Americans.* Their most significant values revolve around the Catholic Church and the family. This is a strong patrilineal society which stresses authority. Younger relatives are subordinate to older; females are subordinate to males; and workers are subordinate to employers. The hierarchy of the church is similar to the hierarchy of social institutions with status playing an important role.

As with the Mormons, the church plays a prominent role in the expression and continuation of values among the Spanish-Americans. The series of direct church linkages from local parish priest to the Pope give a stability to their value systems.

The Spanish-Americans tend to accept nature with little attempt to control it. Their important concept of time is the present, with the past a mere memory. The future is equally vague. They feel that working too hard or worrying about the future is foolish. They accept philosophically that not all of the years will be good, not all of the seeds will sprout, and not all of the children will live. Life in the present, with its excitement and vitality, should be the main concern. Attempting to alter the course of natural events, like rainfall, is considered a useless activity.

*Texans.* They live on homestead land scattered over the region. Strong believers in individual work, they have little community organization and tend to live in relative isolation on separate farms. Their life focuses on individual farmers and their families. Churches have some importance, but there are many competing Protestant denominations.

Social status and economic power are related, and therefore the Texans compete for wealth and prestige. They don't understand why other groups wish to live close together in villages under the control of employers or church officers. The Texan group strives to be independent and its members desire to be their own bosses.

Time, for the Texans, is future-oriented. The past can be forgotten and the present is seen as part of a move toward the future. Thus, the strong belief in "progress," including control over nature. Nature should be exploited, they believe, to provide proper comforts for humans. Modern farming equipment and agricultural technology are considered good. The Texans support artificial rainmaking and other such answers to drought.

This study was reported by Professors Vogt and Roberts in 1956. What changes have occurred in the United States since then that might affect their findings? What changes in values would you expect to observe among the same groups today? Has time been too short for any significant changes? To what extent do you think the characteristics noted for each group were, or are, accurate? Could the social scientists have been reporting only those behaviors that fit their own cultural traditions? How might a Zuñi, Navaho, Mormon, Spanish-American, or Texan have reported the same observations?

## Change in American Values

Things change, yet there is continuity in social life. People change, times change, fashions change. But what about national values? Have American ideas about what is right, good, just, and proper remained the same?

Thomas Jefferson's view of American values included a dominance of individuality. Presumably, only the daring and adventurous were drawn to explore the new world. Individual resourcefulness was a necessity in coping with settlement life and the westward expansion. Separate and often widely isolated families tilled the soil. Individuals sought personal riches by exploration and development. Self-reliance was preached in communities, schools, and churches. The economic system described by Adam Smith, and adopted in America, rested on individual initiative and free enterprise. Jefferson's model for America was a mixture of individual liberty and equality. He envisioned Americans as staunchly independent with strong ideals of equality among individuals.

Historian Frederick Jackson Turner presented an essay in 1893 which is still discussed among historians. The famous "Turner Thesis" that America's unique environment of virtually limitless free and open land explains why this country developed the way it did, supported the Jeffersonian concept of individualistic enterprise and belief in democracy.

Alexis De Tocqueville, a French aristocrat, spent several months observing America in the 1830s and subsequently wrote a two-volume work still used as a source book in the study of American character. His view of America differed markedly from Jefferson's and Turner's. He condemned individualism with such statements as:

> . . . Individualism is a mature and calm feeling, which disposes each member of the community to sever himself from the mass of his fellow-creatures; and to draw apart with his family and his friends; so that, after he has thus formed a little circle of his own, he willingly leaves society at large to itself. Egotism originates in blind instinct: individualism proceeds from erroneous judgment more than from depraved feelings; it originates as much in the deficiencies of the mind as in the perversity of the heart. Egotism blights the germ of all virtue; individualism, at first, only saps the virtues of public life; but, in the long run,

it attacks and destroys all others, and is at length absorbed in downright egotism. Egotism is a vice as old as the world, which does not belong to one form of society more than to another: individualism is of democratic origin, and it threatens to spread in the same ratio as the equality of conditions.

De Tocqueville goes on to describe how the conditions of individualism and equality lead to one's vulnerability to mass opinion because there are no authorities. He says, "I know of no country in which there is so little true independence of mind and freedom of discussion as in America." To De Tocqueville, Americans were conformists, not individualists.

David Riesman, professor of social relations at Harvard, wrote *The Lonely Crowd: A Study of the Changing American Character*, in collaboration with Nathan Glazer and Reuel Denny. This 1950 book argues that a major change has occurred in the character of Americans, and that such change is continuing. His view is that there are two general types of people, inner-directed and other-directed.

The inner-directed type, according to Riesman, has clear, personal goals which are developed early in childhood and which guide his conduct through life. He refers to these individuals as moralizers since they are instilled with a strong sense of morality from their parents.

The other-directed type tunes in to an environment, using signals from others to guide conduct. Riesman calls these individuals inside dopesters since their sense of right and wrong depends on developing situations. Peer influence is of most importance to the other-directed individual.

Riesman states that most people are combinations of inner- and other-directed, with no pure form of either. Yet people can be understood in terms of which is stronger in their character. The change Riesman observes in both character types is partner to alteration in society. Nineteenth-century Americans, says Riesman, were mainly inner-directed, with a strong sense of right and wrong, good and bad. This national mood led to things like the freeing of slaves, the expansion of education, and prison reform—all on moral grounds. It also, presumably, led to censorship, excessive concern for manners and etiquette, and strict enforcement of laws. With such forces as mass media, advertising, and other propaganda keyed to a twentieth-century industrialized consumer society, the character of Americans has shifted from inner direction to responsiveness to others. A concern for getting along, having the right clothes, and being a part of the in crowd is dominant.

Since Riesman's book appeared over two decades ago, have there been any changes in national character? Riesman relates much of the change from inner to other direction to the changes in technology. What technological changes have occurred since 1950 that could be related to any changes in American values?

Theodore Roszak, historian and author of *The Making of a Counter-Culture*, proposes the view that the values resulting from the scientific revolution in the seventeenth century led to a technocratic society with excessive reliance on technology and bureaucracy. He argues that these dominant values are now being challenged by a coalition of young people with radically different ideas. This counterculture is concerned with the alienation that results from assembly-line society; it includes ideas from oriental mysticism, psychedelic drugs, and communal living; and it opposes what it feels are American values of science, technology, and consumption.

Is there indeed a counterculture developing? Which values would be changed and which would remain if a counterculture became dominant in American society?

In a November 1973 Gallup poll, over 70 percent of those interviewed said they were dissatisfied with the honesty and behavior standards of Americans. Only 26 percent were satisfied with the way the country was being governed, and about 55 percent expressed satisfaction with the future for America.

Another Gallup poll, in October 1973, which compared the responses of youth in eleven different countries, found that 80 percent of those interviewed in the United States disagreed with the idea that human nature is fundamentally bad. In the same survey it was found that the value most desired by American youth was "sincerity and love between myself and others." Over 60 percent selected that value, while less than 10 percent selected such values as money and status, a worthwhile job, salvation through faith, freedom from restrictions, devotion to the nation, and devotion to international cooperation. When asked to identify the most important thing that the United States could do at this time, 55 percent of the American youth replied, "to build a peaceful society"; 17 percent thought security was most important; 12 percent selected emphasis on industry and economic growth; 10 percent were for the protection of nature; and 4 percent identified traditions and culture as most important.

Do the values expressed by these groups suggest confusion? Is there value conflict or just misunderstanding about the terms used to convey the values? Are values changing?

**Further Readings**

Angell, Robert. *Free Society and Moral Crisis*, Ann Arbor, Mich.: University of Michigan Press, 1958.

Bronfenbrenner, Urie. "The Mirror Image in Soviet-American Relations," *Journal of Social Issues*, Vol. 17, No. 3, 1961.

Buchanan, Wm., and Cantril, Hadley. *How Nations See Each Other*. UNESCO, 1953.

Cable, Mary. *American Manners and Morals*. New York: American Heritage Publishing Co., 1969.

Glock, Charles, and Siegelman, Ellen. *Prejudice, USA*. New York: Praeger, 1969.

Hayden, Tom. "The Politics of the Movement," in *Radical Ideas and the Schools*, ed. by Nelson, Carlson, & Linton. New York: Holt, Rinehart & Winston, 1972.

Kurtz, Stephen. *Wasteland: Building the American Dream*. New York: Praeger, 1973.

McGiffert, Michael. *The Character of Americans*. Homewood, Ill.: The Dorsey Press, 1964.

Paul, Jon and Charlotte. *Fire: Reports from the Underground Press*. New York: Dutton, 1970.

Roszak, Theodore. *The Making of a Counter-Culture*, Garden City, N.Y.: Doubleday, 1968, 1969.

Sartre, Jean-Paul. "Individualism and Conformism in the United States," *Literary and Philosophical Essays*, New York: Criterion, 1955.

Slater, Philip. *The Pursuit of Loneliness*. Boston: Beacon Press, 1970.

Weiss, Richard. *The American Myth of Success*. New York: Basic Books, 1969.

Westin, Alan, et al. *Views of America*. New York: Harcourt, Brace & World, 1966.

Williams, Robin. *American Society*. New York: Knopf, 1961.

# Chapter 8

# Futuristic Scenarios

### Under Control

"Jerry, get up! I hear something in front of the house. It sounds like car doors closing. What time is it?"

"Huh? What do you want? It's . . . uh . . . about 3:30. What car doors?"

"Listen. There are voices coming closer to the house."

"I'll go downstairs to find out what's happening. Who could be coming here at this time of the morning?"

Jerry Simpson gathered his robe and fumbled for the light switch. The brightness made him blink. As he reached the top of the stairs he heard the door latch rattle.

"Hold on, I'll be there in a minute."

Before he could make it to the door, Jerry heard a key turn in the lock and the snap of the catch. There, playing flashlight beams about the room, stood three or four peace-force officers. The dancing lights made it difficult to count the number. The first officer into the room pointed his beam in Jerry's face and said, "Are you Gerald Simpson?"

"Yes. What do you want?"

"Never mind. Who else is in the house?"

"Only my wife. She's upstairs in bed."

"Jenkins, take Billings upstairs to search. And bring Mrs. Simpson down here to the dining room."

"What are you searching for?" Jerry's voice was starting to quaver. "I'm not a criminal."

"We'll see. Now, sit at the dining table, keep your hands on top, and stop asking questions."

When one of them turned the room lights on, Jerry could see that there were five officers. The one who had been speaking was apparently in charge. She ordered the others to fan out through the house. The officer called Jenkins appeared on the stairs holding Ruth Simpson's arm, directing her into the dining room.

"Jerry, what is happening? Who are these officers? What are they doing here?" Ruth sounded more angered than fearful. "They're going through our dressers, and pulling things off the shelves."

"I don't know, Ruth. They won't answer any questions."

The officer in charge spoke again. "Sit at the table, Mrs. Simpson, and don't ask questions."

A voice from another room called out, "Sergeant Davis! I think I've found some of the books."

Davis, the one in charge, answered, "Be right there. Caldwell, stay here and keep an eye on the Simpsons."

"What books? Why are you looking for books?" Jerry was starting to fidget nervously.

"Shut up! You heard Sergeant Davis tell you 'no questions,' and she means it."

In the next room Davis and another officer were methodically going through bookshelves, taking out each book, scanning the contents, thumbing the pages, and dropping them on the floor. After going through seven or eight books, the officer pushed a book at Davis and pointed at some photographs. Davis nodded, and the book was tossed on a chair. This happened several times, and the pile of books on the chair increased in size.

Jenkins came into the room. "Billings is finishing upstairs. We found a few books on a nightstand and some under the bed. I'm going into the basement now with Caldwell. Officer Brown has relieved him of watching the Simpsons."

"Good. We'll be through here in just a few minutes. Can you imagine leaving these books on open bookshelves?" Davis pointed at the stack on the chair.

Jenkins walked over, picked one up and glanced at it. "Some people are plain stupid. We'll cover the basement now and come back to help you carry this stuff out."

Ruth Simpson had been crying, but was now sitting slumped in the chair, tired and angry. Jerry had been listening to the noise of searchers going through the rooms, and the thud of books hitting the floor. He was agitated, but quiet. Once in a while he and Ruth would exchange startled looks.

Jenkins came bounding up the basement stairs holding a carton. "Sergeant Davis! . . . Sergeant Davis! I've got a gold mine. There are old newspapers and magazines here. We found them in a trunk under the basement stairs."

Jenkins opened the carton and pulled out a faded and brittle magazine with curled edges. As he turned it toward Davis the title *LIFE* stood out on the cover. "It's a 1968 issue of some old magazine. Full of pictures and sappy stories about political conventions and demonstrators. That's enough to put them away for awhile. But, there's even better stuff. Newspapers and pamphlets with articles about student riots and strikes and liberation movements. I haven't gone through all of it yet, but I did find a couple of copies of a rag called *Civil Liberties*. It's hilarious. Just wait until this shows up at the station."

Davis smiled and nodded her head enthusiastically. "I think we've got them now. Let's pack all of it in the van and get the Simpsons down to the station. Have Caldwell help get the books from the next room and call up to Billings to get his take down here. Brown and I will take the Simpsons down with us. This looks like a big one."

Handcuffed and still clad in sleeping garments, Jerry and Ruth Simpson stood bewildered before a large desk as an officer, wearing an impressive uniform with sleeve stripes and gold braid, prepared a video tape machine. It was 7:30 A.M. The officer—the name plate on the desk read Cadre Commander Zink—was preparing to video tape Jerry and Ruth as they answered questions.

"Remember to speak up when I address you," Zink was saying, "and no side comments. Answer each question directly and completely, and don't add irrelevant information. Now then, what are your names?"

"Gerald P. Simpson."

"Ruth R. Simpson."

"Mr. Simpson, do you occupy the house at 371 Forest Drive?"

"Yes, I have a four-month renewable lease from the government. We've been there over three years."

"Are you aware that you are responsible for everything that occurs in that house?"

"Yes, but I don't know what I'm charged with."

"Limit your answers to the questions. Where did you get the books found by Sergeant Davis and her task force?"

"I bought some and borrowed some for my work."

"The occupation you've been assigned is school teacher.

There is no need for you to have any books except those given to you by the officials. That would be two books per year. Everything else to be taught is on television tape and program machine. You had no license to obtain the kinds of books found in your house. Where did you get them?"

"I told you. I bought some and borrowed some. The school censor is a friend of someone in the National Censor's Office, and these books were considered noncontroversial because of their age. I wanted something to enrich my classes."

"That is not your decision to make. The names of the censor and friend—what are they?"

"It wasn't their fault. I kept pestering until they let me have some of the books. I don't want to . . ."

"Simpson, you try my patience. Give me the names immediately, or I'll call an attendant to administer the injection."

"Paul Redmond and Sarah Conn."

"Fine. Now why did you have the box of old magazines and newspapers?"

"They belonged to my father. He had put them in a trunk, and I merely kept them as a remembrance."

"Why didn't you turn them in during one of the clean-up drives to eliminate such rubbish?"

"They were among the few things I had left from my family after the Public Safety Constitution took effect in 1987. It was only nostalgia. The search teams usually passed over the trunk because it was old and dilapidated. I only looked at the stuff inside once in a while."

"That is an additional crime. But, you still have responsibility for having such materials in your house. Mrs. Simpson, were you aware of these books and papers?"

"Yes, the books, but I never read them. I thought they were teaching books for Jerry. I didn't know about the newspapers. What do they say?"

"We are here to ask, not answer, questions. Do you swear that you have never read any of the materials we took from your house?"

"I do. Jerry is such a dedicated teacher he is always trying to find interesting things for his class. My assigned occupation as a plastics carpenter at the new monorail terminal keeps me too busy during the day and too tired at night to do any reading. I wish I could, but I figure Jerry does enough for both of us."

Zink's eyes hardened a bit. "Do you read a lot, Mr. Simpson?"

"Yes. I think it is part of my job."

"Where did you learn to read?"

"At the reading center, with all the other children. My father helped me, too."

"Your father seems very influential. I see by your record that he was given motivational training at the technical institute in Toledo and was relocated near Temple, Texas. Have you heard from him since?"

"No, . . . I understand he tried to contact us a couple of times, and I've made repeated attempts to get a travel permit to see him, but no success yet. Our phone and mail license extends only 100 miles. Since he is the only remaining member of my family, I'd like to get a chance to see him again."

"With this on your record there is little chance of that. You are exhibiting tendencies similar to those of your father. He, apparently, was a member of subversive groups in his youth. So were many disoriented people then. It was a period of chaos. Thankfully, the National Reform Council was able to take the reins of government in 1983 and get the Public Safety Constitution verified and into operation in four years. That was the real founding of our present safe society. In the past fifteen years we have made great strides in controlling crime, pollution, pornography, traffic, urban decay, violence, and many other social problems. Your father, according to this family history, did not share the same ideals as the Council, and did not respond well to our moral reconditioning program. He had to be put into motivational training. Your behaviors in this incident lead me to believe that you have not had your values modified sufficiently."

Jerry shifted his position and cleared his throat. "What do you mean?"

"It is clear that you need a treatment similar to your father's. The safe society cannot permit you to read what you desire, perhaps even teach things not prescribed. You have demonstrated not only a lack of suitable judgment, but also a loss of values necessary for the good of our society. You have involved two censors in this act, for which they will get suitable punishment, and implicated your wife. We will have to test her to find the truth about her statements. You will be programmed into early moral reconditioning at the Kansas City Office, and then a new occupation will be assigned. If you don't respond well at that time, you can expect to go to motivational training."

Jerry was stunned. "I'm not a criminal! Why must I be sent away? How can I appeal this decision?"

Cadre Commander Zink was shocked. His face flushed. He mashed the button which called the attendants, and shouted,

"Aha! You have read the materials in the carton! Among the old magazines and newspapers we found a copy of that fuzzy-minded Bill of Rights that was declared treasonous propaganda by the Council, and pages torn from an old law book like the ones burned during the Freedom Festivals. When you asked about appeal you betrayed yourself. Nowhere in our system do you find such socially destructive terms used. The video recording now has your entire confession. You will be watched closely from now on. Attendants! Take them away."

### Public Hearing

*Transcript of a Public Hearing on Section IV of the Proposed Constitution of the United States Revised*

Hearing Held March 13, 2004
Washington, D.C.
Hearing Board Assembled:
    Honorable Bascom Roberts, Minnesota, Presiding
    Honorable Frederick Sigmaer, Kansas
    Honorable Harold Isberg, Colorado
    Honorable Barbara Kirkland, Oregon
    Honorable Quentin Durham, Virginia
    Franklin Names II, Esq., Counsel to Committee

Roberts: This Hearing Board, convened to consider public opinion regarding the proposed revision of the United States Constitution, is hereby open for session Number 27. Under power vested in this Board by act of the United States Congress, November 18, 2003, witnesses may be called or may request to be heard on matters related to Section IV of the proposed revision. That section refers to protection of the rights of the person. The first witness to be heard this session is Ms. Dorothy Zandel. Ms. Zandel, please identify yourself and your affiliation, then you may proceed.

Zandel: My name is Dorothy M. Zandel. I represent Consumers Amalgamated, and speak in their behalf. Since I have already submitted a written statement to the Board, may I briefly summarize our position regarding the protection clause proposed, and then respond to questions?

Roberts: Certainly.

Zandel: Thank you. Consumers throughout America are caught in a major dilemma as a result of the proposed Section IV. It incorporates the strongest protection language for individual rights of any recommendations in the Revised

Constitution. The phrasing—"Rights of the individual shall be considered paramount in the determination of public good, justice, and opportunity. Infringement of these rights by law or institution shall not be permitted, and means for adjudication of disputes involving individual rights shall be freely provided for all citizens"—contains strong language, but also ambiguity.

The individual consumer would, presumably, have protection against unscrupulous business organizations. But what about the individual businesswoman? Would she have the right to overcharge or give short weight or falsely advertise? How do we decide which individual has superior rights?

Also, when it comes to individual services, like medical doctors, lawyers, and accountants, who has higher level rights? The professional or the client?

A third concern we have is who is going to enforce the guaranteed rights and the means of adjudication? When some regions abolish police forces and formal court proceedings, how will the constitutional rights be maintained?

Finally, since Consumers Amalgamated is affiliated with the Association of the Poor, Urban CARE, Farmworkers Alliance, and the Nader Network, we have a responsibility to echo their great dissatisfaction with other parts of the proposed revision in the constitution which threaten the very framework of a democracy. While we can, with some modifications, agree to Section IV on individual rights, we cannot support the intention to abolish regulatory powers of the government, the creation of regional corridors, or the movement to local authority on such issues as population control, income security, health, and consumer protection. We must be vigilant in our . . .

Sigmaer: Congressman Roberts, we are not convened to hear testimony on other parts of the proposal. In order to provide time to other witnesses, we cannot permit extraneous outbursts. Please request the witness to confine her remarks to Section IV.

Roberts: I am sorry, Ms. Zandel, our Board is to consider only Section IV, and Congressman Sigmaer is perfectly justified in calling my attention to that fact. Please confine your remarks to that portion.

Names: As special counsel to this hearing board, I must agree with Mr. Roberts' interpretation. This board has the specific responsibility to render a report on Section IV, and no other. In the interests of public information, however, it might be valuable if one of the hearing board members would outline some of the provisions of the proposed constitution that directly relate to Section IV. This would not be testimony, but explanation.

Roberts: That is a sensible idea. Ms. Kirkland, since you were one of the co-sponsors of the bill calling for these hearings, would you briefly explain the general plan of the new constitution and show its relation to Section IV.

Kirkland: It would be my pleasure. Although it would take considerable time to cover adequately all aspects of the proposed revision, I can present the rationale for revising and some of the main features of the proposal.

As a result of debate and discussion during periods of social stress in twentieth-century America, two main views of democratic government arose. One called for strengthening the central government in order to have that government control social problems more effectively, and the other called for emphasis on individual rights and responsibilities and a gradual decline in all governmental functions. During the last twenty-five years those debates, as is well known, reached the point where only a revised constitution would break the stalemate.

Movement toward centralized power had created opportunities for massive corruption and political manipulation. The Teapot Dome and Watergate scandals were early indicators, but the 1991 discovery of the Fairmont Plan, and the resulting trials, brought government to a virtual standstill. The same powers that had created such good programs as social security, national health care, free education, and nondiscrimination legislation were being used by segments of business, unions, and the military to prevent any changes from occurring. The result was an outcry for limiting power and increasing individual rights.

At the same time the advocates of individual liberty had succeeded in breaking down such social institutions as health care, the schools, and, in large measure, the standard concept of family. Because the individualists had effectively frustrated the courts, there emerged a pattern in government whereby legislation was proposed but never passed because of fear that either the centralists would oppose it or the individualists would produce injunctions against its operation. Thus, the stalemate and increasing calls for a new constitution to resolve the problem.

Roberts: We appreciate the short lesson on history, Ms. Kirkland, but we must move on through our testimony. Can you very briefly outline the proposal?

Kirkland: Very well. The basic premise in the revised constitution is to provide greater individual liberties and the decentralization of government. This is to be done gradually over a 15-year period so that social order can be maintained during the process. Central government will be limited to coordination among regions. Regional corridors of states which share political views will be established to provide only basic services and communication with other regions.

Local authority to judge disputes between individuals, make decisions on population control, environmental issues, public health, consumer protection, and the like will become the practice as the regional corridors and the states give more powers back to small communities within Metro areas. Corporations, unions, and associations will be required to grant authority for most decisions to local branches and no financial support from those branches will be permitted to go to regional or national offices.

Following the decline of central, then regional, and then state powers over this period, and the increase in individual choices regarding marriage, housing, taxes, schooling, police, and other matters, the Control Commission that would be established to supervise this transition would certify its accomplishment. Then Section IV of the revision would be in force as the basic principle of the society. In any case, at the end of 15 years Section IV would become operative.

If I may, I would like to explain the values that lie behind this proposal.

Durham: That is absurd! We do not have to hear more of the philosophy. The details are bad enough. Where will people get jobs, bank money, be safe from criminals, learn skills, or any of the normal social obligations we have to each other? This plan is a conspiracy to destroy our country and humanity. It will put us back in a jungle.

Roberts: Order! Order!

Durham: Under the proposal you could not call for order! I would have the right to punch you in the mouth.

Roberts: I call for order to get the hearing underway!

Durham: I will not be silent when my country is at stake! I demand that . . .

Roberts: I declare this session adjourned.

## Chapter 9

# Activities and Selected Resource Materials

### Activities

1. Studies done in 1970 by CBS News and reported in *Public Opinion* by Robert Chandler indicated that a majority of adults surveyed across the United States would be willing to restrict some of the basic freedoms contained in the Bill of Rights. For example, 76 percent of those interviewed believed that extremist groups should not be permitted to organize demonstrations against the government, even when there was no apparent threat of violence. Fifty-eight percent felt that police should be allowed to hold a person who is suspected of a serious crime until there is enough evidence to prefer charges. About 55 percent indicated that newspapers, radio, and TV should not be permitted to report some stories considered by the government to be harmful to the national interests even when there was no wartime censorship.

1.1 Examine the Bill of Rights as a statement of United States values. Discuss reasons for differing views on the values.

1.2 Prepare a questionnaire based on the Bill of Rights, using examples of contemporary events. Use the questionnaire to survey students and other members of the community anonymously, then compare responses.

1.3 Investigate reports of United States Supreme Court cases related to aspects of the Bill of Rights to identify values involved, value conflicts, and how they are resolved.

1.4 Develop a scale to measure the differences among values in terms of actual choices made in public affairs. A sam-

## 114  *Values and Society*

ple item might be: *Freedom of the press*

| No limits | Few | Several | Many | Total control |
| --- | --- | --- | --- | --- |

Examine news stories to find examples of decisions being made that can be measured on the scale. Visit public meetings of community groups—city council, board of education, planning board, etc.—and rate group decisions and policies according to the scale.

2. Go back over Chapters 2 and 3 and design different exercises which show the relation between language and values.

2.1 Try to write one paragraph using words of low-intensity values and another paragraph using high-intensity value-laden words. Discuss the same topic in both paragraphs.

2.2 Collect and compare examples of language used in conveying values—advertising, news stories, TV interviews, etc. Look for stereotype thinking and labeling.

3. Identify the major social institutions in your community which have affected your value system. Interview people who you think represent these institutions, like parents for family; teachers for school; religious leaders; friends for peer group. Ask their views on values such as cooperation, competition, honesty, integrity, relations with the environment, rights of minorities, authority, responsibility, and others. Compare the results. How do they differ? Why?

4. Observe television programs for a period of time and note the values conveyed. Pay special attention to the commercials; the advertising business depends upon its ability to persuade you. Keep track of the values portrayed on television, noting such factors as:

1. frequency of presentation
2. means of conveying value
    a. by spoken words
    b. by printed words
    c. by other symbols
    d. by gestures and facial expressions
    e. by sounds
    f. others
3. techniques of persuasion
    a. association with other positive values
        "Be popular; use Zap toothpaste." Popularity is the positive value.

b. comparison with others
"Of all headache remedies, the only brand that contains broxyl vinalate, a special ingredient approved by doctors." Appeal to the American belief in science and medicine
c. opposition to negative social values
"Don't be embarrassed by S.O. (skin odor); rub Flasho all over your body and enjoy 11-hour protection from the heartache of S.O." Human odors perceived as negative.
d. identification with social status values
"People of distinction agree on the new, luxury model Pinnacle 8 automobile—designed in good taste for people who know quality and accept only the best."

4.1 Read the weekly television guide. What comments about American values can be inferred from that listing?

4.2 Examine a popular newspaper or magazine to see how much space is devoted to differing kinds of material—local, national, and international news, household information, advertising, feature stories, comics, obituaries, etc. Where do the editors place those items considered to be of highest value? How do you know?

**5.** Visit the local courthouse or city hall to obtain information from the census on the diversity of people living in your community. Which are the largest groups? Which are smallest? Where do the various groups live?

5.1 Visit sections of the community which have ethnic characteristics. What signs and symbols of that identification are observable? What are the apparent similarities with other community groups?

5.2 Establish a student exchange program for a day, a week, or longer with a school nearby that has different subcultual groups in attendance. What similarities and differences in viewpoint exist?

**6.** Survey local residents to determine their views on the nature of the American character. Ask what they consider basic American values to be, and what a typical American would say or do in different situations. Use some of the ideas in Chapter 7 to prepare an interview sheet on American values.

**7.** Write your own futuristic scenario to describe American society about the year 2000.

## Films

*Doubleday Multimedia*

World in Transition Series: *Who Owns the Moon?*, *Don't Crowd Me*, *Who Owns the Bottom of the Ocean?*, *Can the World Be Fed?*, *Is Gold Obsolete?* (about 15 min. each, color)

*Encyclopedia Britannica Films or McGraw-Hill Films*

*Tumult, Turmoil, Turbulence.* Civil rights movement. (13 min., B/W)
*The Trouble with Chinatown.* Immigration and westernization. (26 min., color)
*State of the Earth.* Essay on the quality of American life. (18 min., color)
*The Orange and the Green.* Separate societies in Ireland. (21 min., color)
*Oh! Woodstock!* Exploration of the generation gap. (26 min., color)
*Music.* Variety in musical choices. (53 min., color)
*Mirror of America.* Washington, D.C., as background for patriotic values. (53 min., color)
*Home Country, USA.* Life in six areas of the U.S. (2 parts, 53 min., color)
*The First Americans.* Tracing the earliest immigrants. (2 parts, 53 min., color)
*Confrontation.* Study of San Francisco State College strike. (81 min., color)
*Control or Destroy.* World population and food. (12 min., B/W)
*CBW: The Secrets of Secrecy.* Explores chemical and biological warfare. (47 min., color)
*Alone in the Midst of the Land.* Dramatization of future environment. (27 min., color)

*International Film Bureau*

*Who Cops Out?* Differing views of adolescents. (11 min., color)

*Learning Corporation of America*

*Searching for Values: A Film Anthology.* Fifteen films edited from commercial feature films to focus on value problems. (about 18 min. each, color & B/W)

## McGraw-Hill Films

*Future Shock.* Based on Toffler's best-selling book. (42 min., color)
*Man of Aran.* Struggle for survival. (77 min., B/W)
*Replay.* Humor in generation-gap comparisons. (8 min., color)
*The Son.* Alienation and values. (10 min., B/W)
*The Hat.* Organization of a peaceful world. (18 min., color)

## Pyramid Films

*The American Time Capsule.* 1,300 scenes in American history in 3 minutes. (color)

## Teleketics Films

*Those Who Mourn.* Explores concepts of death and personal loss. (5 min., B/W)

## Oxford Films

*Latino: A Cultural Conflict.* Illustrates problems of Spanish-speaking student in U.S. (21 min., color)
*Great American Patriotic Speeches.* Patrick Henry, Washington, Lincoln. (3 films, 15 min. each, color)
*Poetry by Americans.* Poe, James Weldon Johnson, Frost, Whitman. (4 films, about 10 min. each, color)
*Values and Goals.* Students defining positions. (28 min., color)

## Wombat Productions

*Joseph Schultz.* Obedience and conflict in a Yugoslavian village. (13 min., color)

### Filmstrips, Records, Multimedia Kits, Film Loops

The following audio-visual aids are available from Social Studies School Service.

*Filmstrips: Regional Cultures of the U.S.*

*America; Changing the System; Human Values Series; The World's Great Religions; The Nation State; The Age of Megaton; Revolution: China and Mexico; Relocation of Japanese-Americans: Right or Wrong?; America's Changing*

118  Values and Society

*Lifestyles; New York Times Filmstrips; Associated Press Special Reports; Rumor Clinic; The Distorted Image; The Other American Minorities; American Woman's Search for Equality; The New American Woman.*

Records

*You Are There
I Can Hear It Now
Civil Disobedience*

Documentary Photo Aids

*Classic American Political Cartoons
Crisis Pictures
The Negro Experience in America*

*Film Loops: Historical Newsreel Highlights Series*

*8mm Documents Project series*

*Multimedia: Peacekeeping Kit*

*Nations of Today Series
La Raza
Man at AQ Kupruk
Patterns of Human Conflict*

*Additional Materials*

The following are available from other distributors, as noted.
*Tradition and Change in Four Societies.* Multimedia. Holt, Rinehart & Winston.
*Men from Earth.* Filmstrip. AIMS Instructional Media.
*They Came to America.* Filmstrip. Audio Visual Narrative Arts.
*Changing Africa.* Multimedia. Interculture Associates.
*Fundamental Freedoms Project* . Multimedia. Xerox Corp.
*Fieldstaff Perspectives.* Multimedia. American Universities Field Staff.
*Man and His World.* Film loop. Hubbard Instructional Media.

*World Communities.* Film loop. Hubbard Instructional Media.
*American Civilization Series.* Filmstrip. Educational Dimensions Corp.
*Protest Writing: An American Tradition.* Filmstrip. Educational Dimensions Corp.
*The Now Generation.* Filmstrip. Educational Dimensions Corp.
*Prejudice.* Filmstrip. Educational Dimensions Corp.

### Simulations, Games

The following are available from Social Studies School Service.
*Star Power.* Simulated multi-level society and power problems.
*Culturecontact.* Conflict potential of differing cultures.
*Guns or Butter.* Illustrates arms race.
*Confrontation.* Simulates Cuban Missile Crisis.
*Humanus.* Social and political decision-making on survival.
*Crisis.* International conflict simulation.
*Plans.* Interest group politics in America.
*Ghetto.* Illustrates frustration, and education as a value.
*Micro-Community.* Long-term simulation on U.S. history.
*Propaganda.* Game dealing with propaganda techniques.
*Nuremberg.* Moral and legal dilemmas in war crimes.
*Disunia.* Futuristic simulation based on U.S. Constitution.

Deborah Tucker
685-8228